AF477245

Glossary for the S-Series IPS specifications

SX001G-B6865-0X000-00

Issue No. 2.1

S-Series IPS specifications
Block release 2021

Usage rights: Refer to SX001G-A-00-00-0000-00A-021A-A

Copyright © 2021 by: AeroSpace and Defense Industries Association of Europe (ASD)

Publishers:

AeroSpace and Defence Industries Association of Europe

Aerospace Industries Association of America (AIA)

Applicable to: All   **SX001G-A-00-00-0000-00A-001A-A**

This specification has been developed by the following organizations (in alphabetic order):

- Airbus Defense & Space   Spain & Germany
- HiCo   Austria
- ISS   United States of America
- Isselnord   Italy
- Nexter Group   France
- Rolls-Royce   United Kingdom
- Pentecom   United States of America
- Saab AB   Sweden
- Sopra Steria   Germany

Editor:
- O'Neil & Associates   United States of America

The following people contributed to the development of this specification (in alphabetic order):

- AUGSBURGER, Ryan
- DAY, Mike
- DE LANGE, Daan
- FLECK, Andreas
- GAMEZ DE LA FUENTE, Daniel
- GYLLSTROM, Leif [#]
- HASLAM, Paul [+]
- MITJANS, Félix [*]
- OWEN, Parker
- PINTER, Andreas
- SOMOZA, Ramón
- TEDESCHI, Stefano

[*] = Chair   [#] = Former Chair   [+] = Editor-in-Chief

Copyright and user agreement

1 Copyright

Copyright © 2014-2021 AeroSpace and Defense Industries Association of Europe - ASD.

All rights reserved. No part of this document may be reproduced or transmitted in any form or by any means, electronic or mechanical, including photocopying and recording, or by any information storage or retrieval system, except as may be expressly permitted by the copyright act or in writing by the publisher.

SX001G™ is a trade mark owned by ASD.

All correspondence and queries should be directed to:

ASD
10 Rue du Trône 100
1050 Brussels
Belgium

2 Agreement for use of the specification SX001G™ suite of information

2.1 Definitions

SX001G™ suite of information means, but is not limited to:

- the Glossary for the S-Series IPS specifications – SX001G
- examples (eg, XML instances, pdf files, style sheets) and schemas
- any other software or information under the heading "**SX001G™ suite of information**", available for download from www.sX000i.org

Copyright holder means AeroSpace and Defense Industries Association of Europe (ASD).

2.2 Notice to user

By using all or any portion of **SX001G™ suite of information** you accept the terms and conditions of this user agreement.

This user agreement is enforceable against you and any legal entity that has obtained **SX0001G™ suite of information** or any portion thereof and on whose behalf it is used.

2.3 License to use

As long as you comply with the terms of this user agreement, the copyright holders grant to you a non-exclusive license to use **SX001G™ suite of information**.

2.4 Intellectual property rights

SX001G™ suite of information is the intellectual property of and is owned by the copyright holder. Except as expressly stated herein, this user agreement does not grant you any intellectual property right in the **SX001G™ suite of information** and all rights not expressly granted are reserved by the copyright holder.

2.5 No modifications

You must not modify, adapt or translate, in whole or in part, **SX001G™ suite of information**.

2.6 No warranty

SX001G™ suite of information is being delivered to you "as is". The copyright holder does not warrant the performance or result you may obtain by using **SX001G™ suite of information**.

The copyright holder makes no warranties, representations or indemnities, express or implied, whether by statute, common law, custom, usage or otherwise as to any matter including without limitation merchantability, integration, satisfactory quality, fitness for any particular purpose, or non-infringement of third parties rights.

2.7 Limitation of liability

In no event will the copyright holder be liable to you for any damages, claims or costs whatsoever or any consequential, indirect or incidental damages, or any lost profits or lost savings or for any claim by a third party, even if the copyright holder has been advised of the possibility of such damages, claims, costs, lost profits or lost savings.

2.8 Indemnity

You agree to defend, indemnify, and hold harmless the copyright holder and its parents and affiliates and all of their employees, agents, directors, officers, proprietors, partners, representatives, shareholders, servants, attorneys, predecessors, successors, assigns, and those who have worked on the preparation, publication or distribution of the **SX001G™ suite of information** from and against any and all claims, proceedings, damages, injuries, liabilities, losses, costs, and expenses (including reasonable attorneys' fees and litigation expenses), relating to or arising from your use of the **SX001G™ suite of information** or any breach by you of this user agreement.

2.9 Governing law and arbitration

This user agreement will be governed by and construed in accordance with the laws of the Kingdom of Belgium.

In the event of any dispute, controversy or claim arising out of or in connection with this user agreement, or the breach, termination or invalidity thereof, the parties agree to submit the matter to settlement proceedings under the ICC (International Chamber of Commerce) ADR rules. If the dispute has not been settled pursuant to the said rules within 45 days following the filing of a request for ADR or within such other period as the parties may agree in writing, such dispute shall be finally settled under the rules of arbitration of the International Chamber of Commerce by three arbitrators appointed in accordance with the said rules of arbitration. All related proceedings should be at the place of the ICC in Paris, France.

The language to be used in the arbitral proceedings shall be English.

Note

The following letter from the Secretary General of ASD extends the special usage rights of this specification and has been included for information, without affecting the technical contents. The content of this letter will be included in the copyright information as part of the S-Series 2024 block release.

Aerospace and Defence
Industries Association of Europe

<u>Special Usage Rights for the S-Series Specifications</u>

To whom it may concern,

This letter seeks to clarify the special usage rights for the suite of documents known as the S-Series Specifications, for which the Aerospace and Defence Industries Association of Europe (ASD) holds the copyright and trademark.

The special usage rights are described as follows:

Permission to use or deliver training from the information contained in the S-Series Specifications, and the right to reproduce or publish the S-Series Specifications, in whole or in part, is hereby given to the following:

1. National Associations who are members of ASD and all their member companies;

2. Members of Aerospace Industries Association of America;

3. Members of the ATA e-Business Program;

4. Members of International Coordinating Council of Aerospace Industries Associations (ICCAIA) not included in categories 1 through 2 inclusively;

5. Airlines and Armed Forces that are customers of Companies included in Categories 1 through 3 inclusively;

6. Ministries of Defence of the member countries of ASD, of NATO and NATO Partners[1];

7. The Department of Defense of the USA;

8. NATO bodies, organizations & agencies;

9. Universities;

10. Technologies and Research Institutes.

Any further requirement for clarification, should in the first instance be directed to the Service Commission of the ASD.

Yours Sincerely,

Jan Pie

Secretary General of ASD

---

[1] as per: https://www.nato.int/cps/en/natohq/51288.htm;

SX001G-A-00-00-0000-00A-021A-A

Page intentionally blank.

SX001G-A-00-00-0000-00A-021A-A   Applicable to: All

End of data module

Highlights

List of tables

References

Table 1 Copyright

Chap No.	Summary of changes
Copyright	ASD address has been changed

Table 2 References

Chap No.	Title
SX002D	Common data model for the S-Series ILS specifications
SX000i	International specification for Integrated Product Support (IPS)

Table 3 Summary

Chap No.	Summary of changes
N/A	The term Integrated Logistics Support (ILS) has been changed to Integrated Product Support (IPS). This change has been introduced to all S-Series IPS specifications

Table 4 Chap 1

Chap No.	Summary of changes
1.1 , 1.2 & 1.4	Updated title of SX000i
1.3	Added Para with clarification on new formatting of attribute and class names

---

Applicable to: All

SX001G-A-00-00-0000-00U-009A-A

Table 5 Chap 2

Chap No.	Summary of changes
All	Highlighted attributes and classes with special format.
Chap 2.1	New Analysis Candidate Item UoF definition
	New `AnalysisActivity` UML class definition
	New `analysisActivityDecision` CDM `ClassificationType` definition
	New `analysisActivityDecisionRationale` CDM `DescriptorType` definition
	New `AnalysisActivityRevision` UML class definition
	New `analysisActivityRevisionDate` CDM `DateType` definition
	New `analysisActivityRevisionIdentifier` CDM `IdentifierType` definition
	New `analysisActivityRevisionRationale` CDM `DescriptorType` definition
	New `analysisActivityRevisionStatus` CDM `StateType` definition
	New `analysisActivityStatusDescription` CDM `DescriptorType` definition
	New `analysisActivityType` CDM `ClassificationType` definition
	New `AnalysisCandidateItem` UML <<extend>> stereotype definition
	New `AnalysisCandidateItemSelectionData` UML class definition
	New `analysisCandidateItemSelectionIndicator` CDM `ClassificationType` definition
	New `analysisCandidateItemSelectionRationale` CDM `DescriptorType` definition
	New `ApplicableDecisionTreeTemplate` UML class definition
	New `AssociatedEnvironmentDefinition` UML class definition
Chap 2.2	New `BaseObject` UML class definition
	Breakdown UoF name changed to Breakdown Structure UoF
	New `breakdownElementChildSequenceNumber` UML string definition
	New `breakdownElementDescription` CDM `DescriptorType` definition
	New `breakdownElementRevisionDate` CDM `DateType` definition
	New `breakdownElementRevisionRationale` CDM `DescriptorType` definition
	New `breakdownElementRevisionRelationshipType` CDM `ClassificationType` definition
	New `breakdownRevisionDate` CDM `DateType` definition
	New `breakdownRevisionRationale` CDM `DescriptorType` definition
	New `BreakdownRevisionRelationship` UML class definition
	New `breakdownRevisionRelationshipType` CDM `ClassificationType` definition

Chap No.	Summary of changes

New definition of "Concession" business term

New Capability Definition UoF definition

New `CapabilityDefinition` UML class definition

New `capabilityDefinitionCategory` CDM `ClassificationType` definition

New `CapabilityDefinitionCharacteristic` UML class definition

New `capabilityDefinitionCharacteristicDescription` CDM `DescriptorType` definition

New `capabilityDefinitionCharacteristicName` CDM `NameType` definition

New `capabilityDefinitionCharacteristicValue` CDM `PropertyType` definition

New `capabilityDefinitionCharacteristicValueComparisonOperator` CDM `ClassificationType` definition

New `capabilityDefinitionDescription` CDM `DescriptorType` definition

New `capabilityDefinitionIdentifier` CDM `IdentifierType` definition

New `CapabilityDefinitionItem` UML <<extend>> stereotype definition

New `capabilityDefinitionName` CDM `NameType` definition

New `CapabilityDefinitionRevision` UML class definition

New `capabilityDefinitionRevisionDate` CDM `DateType` definition

New `capabilityDefinitionRevisionIdentifier` CDM `IdentifierType` definition

New `capabilityDefinitionRevisionRationale` CDM `DescriptorType` definition

New `capabilityDefinitionRevisionStatus` CDM `StateType` definition

New Circuit Breaker UoF definition

New `circuitBreakerLocationDescription` CDM `DescriptorType` definition

New `CircuitBreakerLocationItem` UML <<select>> stereotype definition

New `conditionTypeAssertMemberAssertValueComparisonOperator` CDM `ClassificationType` definition

New Concession Business Term definition

New `contractItemDetailsContractQuantity` CDM `PropertyType` definition

New `Country` UML class definition

New `countryName` CDM `NameType` definition

Chap No.	Summary of changes
Chap 2.4	New Damage Definition UoF definition
	New `DamageAnalysis` UML class definition
	New `DamageAnalysisRevision` UML class definition
	New `DamageCause` UML class definition
	New `DamageDefinition` UML class definition
	New damageDefinitionDescription CDM `DescriptorType` definition
	New damageDefinitionFamily CDM `ClassificationType` definition
	New damageDefinitionName CDM `NameType` definition
	New `DamageImpact` UML class definition
	New damageImpactRatio CDM `PropertyType` definition
	New Decision Tree Template Definition UoF definition
	New `DecisionTreeAnalysisItem` UML <<extend>> stereotype definition
	New `DecisionTreeTemplate` UML class definition
	New `DecisionTreeTemplateActionDefinition` UML class definition
	New decisionTreeTemplateActionDefinitionDescription CDM `DescriptorType` definition
	New decisionTreeTemplateActionDefinitionIdentifier CDM `IdentifierType` definition
	New decisionTreeTemplateActionDefinitionName CDM `NameType` definition
	New decisionTreeTemplateAnalysisDomain CDM `NameType` definition
	New decisionTreeTemplateDescription CDM `DescriptorType` definition
	New `DecisionTreeTemplateEndActionDefinition` UML class definition
	New `DecisionTreeTemplateFollowOnItem` UML <<select>> stereotype definition
	New `DecisionTreeTemplateFurtherAnalysisActionDefinition` UML class definition
	New decisionTreeTemplateIdentifier CDM `IdentifierType` definition
	New decisionTreeTemplateName CDM `NameType` definition
	New `DecisionTreeTemplateQuestionDefinition` UML class definition
	New decisionTreeTemplateQuestionDefinitionDescription CDM `DescriptorType` definition
	New decisionTreeTemplateQuestionDefinitionIdentifier CDM `IdentifierType` definition
	New decisionTreeTemplateQuestionDefinitionName CDM `NameType` definition
	New `DecisionTreeTemplateRevision` UML class definition
	New decisionTreeTemplateRevisionDate CDM `DateType` definition
	New decisionTreeTemplateRevisionIdentifier CDM `IdentifierType` definition

SX001G-A-00-00-0000-00A-00UA-A   Applicable to: All

Chap No.	Summary of changes
	New `decisionTreeTemplateRevisionRationale` **CDM** `DescriptorType` **definition**
	New `decisionTreeTemplateRevisionStatus` **CDM** `StateType` **definition**
	New `DecisionTreeTemplateStartItem` **UML <<select>> stereotype definition**
	New **diameter CDM** `PropertyType` **definition**
	New `documentIssueRationale` **CDM** `DescriptorType` **definition**
	New `documentIssueStatus` **CDM** `StateType` **definition**
<u>Chap 2.5</u>	New **Environment Definition UoF definition**
	New `EnvironmentDefinition` **UML class definition**
	New `EnvironmentDefinitionCharacteristic` **UML class definition**
	New `environmentDefinitionCharacteristicDescription` **CDM** `DescriptorType` **definition**
	New `environmentDefinitionCharacteristicName` **CDM** `NameType` **definition**
	New `environmentDefinitionCharacteristicValue` **CDM** `PropertyType` **definition**
	New `environmentDefinitionCharacteristicValueComparisonOperator` **CDM** `ClassificationType` **definition**
	New `environmentDefinitionDescription` **CDM** `DescriptorType` **definition**
	New `environmentDefinitionIdentifier` **CDM** `IdentifierType` **definition**
	New `EnvironmentDefinitionItem` **UML <<extend>> stereotype definition**
	New `environmentDefinitionName` **CDM** `NameType` **definition**
	New `EnvironmentDefinitionRelationship` **UML class definition**
	New `environmentDefinitionRelationshipType` **CDM** `ClassificationType` **definition**
	New `EnvironmentDefinitionRevision` **UML class definition**
	New `environmentDefinitionRevisionDate` **CDM** `DateType` **definition**
	New `environmentDefinitionRevisionIdentifier` **CDM** `IdentifierType` **definition**
	New `environmentDefinitionRevisionRationale` **CDM** `DescriptorType` **definition**
	New `environmentDefinitionRevisionStatus` **CDM** `StateType` **definition**
	New `extensionCode` **UML string definition**
	New `extensionProducer` **UML string definition**

Chap No.	Summary of changes
Chap 2.6	New `FacilityLocation` UML class definition
	New `facilityLocationIdentifier` CDM `IdentifierType` definition
	New `facilityLocationPeriod` CDM `DateRange` definition
	New `FacilityRelationship` UML class definition
	New `facilityRelationshipType` CDM `ClassificationType` definition
	New Failure Mode UoF definition
	New `FailureMode` UML class definition
	New `FailureModeAnalysis` UML class definition
	New `failureModeAnalysisDescription` CDM `DescriptorType` definition
	New `FailureModeAnalysisItem` UML <<extend>> stereotype definition
	New `FailureModeAnalysisRevision` UML class definition
	New `failureModeAnalysisRevisionDate` CDM `DateType` definition
	New `failureModeAnalysisRevisionIdentifier` CDM `IdentifierType` definition
	New `failureModeAnalysisRevisionRationale` CDM `DescriptorType` definition
	New `failureModeAnalysisRevisionStatus` CDM `StateType` definition
	New `failureModeAnalysisType` CDM `ClassificationType` definition
	New `FailureModeCause` UML class definition
	New `failureModeCauseDescription` CDM `DescriptorType` definition
	New `failureModeCauseIdentifier` CDM `IdentifierType` definition
	New `FailureModeCauseItem` UML <<select>> stereotype definition
	New `FailureModeCauseItemRelationship` UML class definition
	New `failureModeCauseItemRelationshipType` CDM `ClassificationType` definition
	New `failureModeCauseRatio` CDM `PropertyType` definition
	New `FailureModeCompensatingProvision` UML class definition
	New `failureModeCompensatingProvisionCategory` CDM `ClassificationType` definition
	New `failureModeCompensatingProvisionDescription` CDM `DescriptorType` definition
	New `failureModeCompensatingProvisionIdentifier` CDM `IdentifierType` definition
	New `failureModeCriticality` CDM `ClassificationType` definition
	New `failureModeDescription` CDM `DescriptorType` definition
	New `FailureModeEffect` UML class definition
	New `failureModeEffectDescription` CDM `DescriptorType` definition
	New `FailureModeEffectItem` UML <<select>> stereotype definition
	New `FailureModeEffectItemRelationship` UML class definition

Chap No.	Summary of changes

New `failureModeEffectLevel` CDM `ClassificationType` definition

New `failureModeEffectName` CDM `NameType` definition

New `failureModeIdentifier` CDM `IdentifierType` definition

New `failureModeName` CDM `NameType` definition

New `failureModeRatio` CDM `PropertyType` definition

New `FinalInServiceOptimizationAnalysisStep` UML class definition

New `FollowOnInServiceOptimizationAnalysis` UML class definition

New `followOnInServiceOptimizationAnalysisRationale` CDM `DescriptorType` definition

New `FurtherAnalysisInServiceOptimizationAnalysisStep` UML class definition

Chap 2.9

New definition of "individual" business term

New definition of "Integrated Logistic Support" business term

New definition of "Integrated Product Support" business term

New definition of "Item" business term

Chap 2.10

New definition of "Job" business term

Chap 2.11

New definition of "Knowledge" business term.

Chap 2.13

New definition of "Maintenance" business term.

New definition of "Military service" business term.

New Measurement Point UoF definition

New Mission Definition UoF definition

New `MissionDefinition` UML class definition

New `missionDefinitionDescription` CDM `DescriptorType` definition

New `missionDefinitionFrequency` CDM `PropertyType` definition

New MissionDefinitionItem UML <<extend>> stereotype definition

New `missionDefinitionName` CDM `NameType` definition

New `missionDefinitionObjective` CDM `DescriptorType` definition

New `MissionDefinitionParty` UML class definition

New `MissionDefinitionPartyItem` UML <<select>> stereotype definition

New `missionDefinitionPartyRole` CDM `ClassificationType` definition

New `MissionDefinitionRelationship` UML class definition

New `missionDefinitionRelationshipType` CDM `ClassificationType` definition New `MissionDefinitionRevision` UML class definition

New `missionDefinitionRevisionDate` CDM `DateType` definition

New `missionDefinitionRevisionIdentifier` CDM `IdentifierType` definition

New `missionDefinitionRevisionRationale` CDM `DescriptorType` definition

New `missionDefinitionRevisionStatus` CDM `StateType` definition

Chap No.	Summary of changes
	New `missionDefinitionType` CDM `ClassificationType` definition
Chap 2.14	New `nameProvidedBy` CDM `Organization` definition
Chap 2.15	New `operatingLocationTypeDescription` CDM `DescriptorType` definition
	New definition of "Occupational background" business term
	New definition of "Original equipment manufacturer" business term
ap 2.16	New definition of "Party" business term.
	New definition of "Person" business term.
	New definition of "Product support" business term
	New `partsListRevisionDate` CDM `DateType` definition
	New `partsListRevisionRationale` CDM `DescriptorType` definition
	New Performance Parameter UoF definition
	New `PerformanceParameter` UML class definition
	New `performanceParameterCalculationMethod` CDM DescriptorType definition
	New `PerformanceParameterItem` UML <<extend>> stereotype definition
	New `PerformanceParameterRevision` UML class definition
	New `performanceParameterRevisionDate` CDM `DateType` definition
	New `performanceParameterRevisionIdentifier` CDM `IdentifierType` definition
	New `performanceParameterRevisionRationale` CDM `DescriptorType` definition
	New `performanceParameterRevisionStatus` CDM `StateType` definition
	New `performanceParameterType` CDM `ClassificationType` definition
	New `performanceParameterValue` CDM `PropertyType` definition
	New `performanceParameterValueFraction` CDM `PropertyType` definition
	New `PerformanceParameterValueGroup` UML class definition
	New `performanceParameterValueLimitQualifier` CDM `ClassificationType` definition
	New Product Usage Phase UoF definition
	New `ProductUsagePhase` UML class definition
	New `productUsagePhaseDescription` CDM `DescriptorType` definition
	New `productUsagePhaseDuration` CDM `PropertyType` definition
	New `ProductUsagePhaseItem` UML <<extend>> stereotype definition
	New `productUsagePhaseName` CDM `NameType` definition
	New `ProductUsagePhaseRelationship` UML class definition
	New `productUsagePhaseRelationshipType` CDM `ClassificationType` definition

SX001G-A-00-00-0000-00A-00UA-A

Applicable to: All

Chap No.	Summary of changes

New `ProjectSpecificAttribute` UML class definition

New `projectSpecificAttributeName` CDM `validValue` definitionNew `ProjectSpecificAttributeValue` UML <<select>> stereotype definition

New `ProjectSpecificExtensionItem` UML <<extend>> stereotype definition

Chap 2.17 — New `QuestionInServiceOptimizationAnalysisStep` UML class definition

Chap 2.18 — New Resource Specification UoF definition

New `ResourceSpecificationRevision` UML class definition

New `resourceSpecificationRevisionDate` CDM `DateType` definition

New `resourceSpecificationRevisionIdentifier` CDM `IdentifierType` definition

New `resourceSpecificationRevisionRationale` CDM `DescriptorType` definition

New `resourceSpecificationRevisionStatus` CDM `StateType` definition

New `resourceSpecificationType` CDM `ClassificationType` definition

Chap 2.19 — New definition of "Service" business term.

New definition of "Skill" business term.

New definition of "Skill level" business term.

New definition of "Supplier" business term.

New definition of "Support concept" business term.

New `securityClassificationAuthority` CDM `Organization` definition

New `SerializedHardwarePartModification` UML class definition

New `serializedHardwarePartModificationDate` CDM `DateType` definition

New Special Event UoF definition

New `SpecialEventAnalysis` UML class definition

New `SpecialEventAnalysisRevision` UML class definition

New `SpecialEventDefinition` UML class definition

New `specialEventDefinitionCauseCategory` CDM `ClassificationType` definition

New `specialEventDefinitionDecription` CDM `DescriptorType` definition

New `specialEventDefinitionName` CDM `NameType` definition

New `specialEventDefinitionOccurrenceValue` CDM `PropertyType` definition

New `specialEventOccurenceRatio` CDM `PropertyType` definition

New `SpecialEventProductUsagePhaseOccurrence` UML class definition

New `SubtaskWarningCautionNote` UML class definition

Chap No.	Summary of changes
Chap 2.20	New definition of "Task requirement" business term.
	New definition of "Task" business term.
	New definition of "Trade" business term.
	New `TaskRequirementJustification` UML class definition
	New `taskRequirementJustificationDescription` CDM DescriptorType definition
	New `TaskRequirementJustificationItem` UML <<select>> stereotype definition
	New `taskRequirementRevisionDate` CDM `DateType` definition
	New `taskRequirementRevisionRationale` CDM `DescriptorType` definition
	New `TaskResourceDefinitionItem` UML <<select>> stereotype definition
	New `taskRevisionDate` CDM `DateType` definition
	New `taskRevisionRationale` CDM `DescriptorType` definition
	New `thresholdValueQualifier` CDM `ClassificationType` definition
Chap 2.21	New definition of "User" business term.
	New `umlBoolean` UML class definition
	New `umlInteger` UML class definition
	New `umlReal` UML class definition
	New `umlString` UML class definition
	New `umlUnlimitedNatural` UML class definition
Chap 2.22	New definition of "Vendor" business term.
Chap 2.23	New definition of "Waiver" business term.
Chap 2.25	Added reference to Chap 2.22

Table of contents

The listed documents are included in Issue 2.1, dated 2021-04-30, of this publication.

Applicable to: All   **SX001G-A-00-00-0000-00A-009A-A**

Chapter	Data module title	Data module code	Applic
Chap 2.24	Glossary - X	SX001G-A-02-24-0000-00A-040A-A	All
Chap 2.25	Glossary - Y	SX001G-A-02-25-0000-00A-040A-A	All
Chap 2.26	Glossary - Z	SX001G-A-02-26-0000-00A-040A-A	All

Chapter 1

Introduction to the specification

Table of contents

Page intentionally blank.

Chapter 1.1

Purpose

Table of contents
Page

List of tables

References

Table 1 References

Chap No./Document No.	Title
S1000D	International specification for technical publications using a common source database
SX000i	International specification for Integrated Product Support (IPS)

1   General

The glossary for the S-Series Integrated Product Support (IPS) specifications is a repository of the terms and their definitions used throughout the S-Series IPS specifications.

2   Purpose

The purpose of the glossary is to provide a consolidated and harmonized set of terms and definitions that are used within each of the individual S-Series IPS specifications. These include both business terms and data item terms. Business terms include concepts that are significant for understanding one or more of the S-Series IPS specifications. Data item terms correspond to the elements defined within the data models of the S-Series IPS specifications.

3   Background

The international aerospace and defense community has, over the past 20 years, invested considerable effort developing specifications in the field of ILS. The work was accomplished by integrated working groups composed of industry and customer organizations in a collaborative environment. Customer organizations included representatives from national ministries and departments of defense from Europe and the United States. Aerospace and defense associations provided guidance and supported the work as required. The structure and functional coverage of these specifications was largely determined by North Atlantic Treaty Organization (NATO) requirements specified during an international workshop in Paris in 1993.

Beginning in 2003, the relationships between supporting industry organizations were formalized through a series of Memorandums of Understanding (MOU). Initially AeroSpace and Defense Industries Association of Europe (ASD) and Aerospace Industries Association (AIA) signed an MOU to jointly develop and maintain S1000D.

In 2010, ASD and AIA signed an MOU to promote a common, interoperable, international suite of integrated logistics support specifications and jointly develop the S-Series IPS specifications. This MOU authorized the formation of the AIA/ASD IPS Spec Council, whose responsibilities include performing liaison between ASD and AIA, developing and maintaining the S-Series IPS specifications, administering joint meetings and identifying additional areas of harmonization.

The need for a consolidated and harmonized glossary of terms and definitions was recognized as a fundamental requirement for the complete S-Series IPS specifications. Its creation and maintenance was assigned to the Data Modeling and Exchange Working Group (DMEWG) and is numbered SX001G to align it with SX000i.

Chapter 1.2

Scope

Table of contents

Page

List of tables

References

Table 1 References

Chap No./Document No.	Title
S1000D	International specification for technical publications using a common source database
S1000X	Input data specification for S1000D
S2000M	International specification for material management - Integrated data processing
S2000X	Input data specification for S2000M
S3000L	International procedure specification for Logistics Support Analysis (LSA)
S3000X	Input data specification for S3000L
S4000P	International specification for developing and continuously improving preventive maintenance
S4000X	Input data specification for S4000P
S5000F	International specification for in-service data feedback
S6000T	International specification for training analysis and design
S6000X	Input data specification for S6000T
SX000i	International specification for Integrated Product Support (IPS)
SX002D	Common data model for the S-Series ILS specifications
SX004G	Unified Modeling Language (UML) model readers' guidance

Chap No./Document No.	Title
SX005G	S-Series IPS specifications XML schema implementation guidance

1 General

SX001G is designed to consolidate all terms and definitions used throughout the S-Series Integrated Product Support (IPS) specifications into a single glossary, which includes both business terms and data item terms. Business terms include concepts that are significant for understanding one or more of the S-Series IPS specifications. Data item terms correspond to elements defined within the data models of the S-Series IPS specifications.

2 Scope

The scope of this issue of SX001G is limited to the terms and definitions of the data items defined in SX002D Common data model for the S-Series IPS specifications and select business terms defined by the S-Series Terminology Task Team.

3 S-Series IPS Specifications

Multiple AeroSpace and Defense Industries Association of Europe (ASD) and Aerospace Industries Association of America (AIA) IPS specifications are currently available or in the process of development, including:

- S1000D - International specification for technical publications using a common source database
- S1000X - Input data specification for S1000D
- S2000M - International specification for material management - Integrated data processing
- S2000X - Input data specification for S2000M
- S3000L - International procedure specification for Logistics Support Analysis (LSA)
- S3000X - Input data specification for S3000L
- S4000P - International specification for developing and continuously improving preventive maintenance
- S4000X - Input data specification for S4000P
- S5000F - International specification for in-service data feedback
- S6000T - International specification for training analysis and design
- S6000X - Input data specification for S6000T
- SX000i - International specification for Integrated Product Support (IPS)
- SX002D - Common data model for the S-Series IPS specifications
- SX004G - Unified Modeling Language (UML) model readers' guidance
- SX005G - S-Series ILS specifications XML schema implementation guidance

Applicable to: All

End of data module

Chapter 1.3

How to use the specification

Table of contents

List of tables

References

Table 1 References

Chap No./Document No.	Title
Chap 1	Introduction to the specification
Chap 2	Glossary
SX002D	Common data model for the S-Series IPS specifications
SX004G	Unified Modeling Language (UML) model readers' guidance

1   General

This chapter gives an overview of the organization of the specification and the fundamental reading rules.

2   Acronyms

Acronyms are included to aid understanding and to minimize duplication. They are included with the terms and definitions used in this specification and are ordered alphabetically based on the acronym. The same acronym is used for all tenses, the possessive case and singular and plural forms of a given word or term.

3   Organization of the specification

3.1   Chapter 1 - Introduction to the specification

Chap 1 provides a summarized view on purpose, background and scope of SX001G.

3.2   Chapter 2 - Glossary

Chap 2 provides the Glossary terms and definitions. Chap 2 is subdivided into a separate subchapter for each letter of the alphabet.

Each term entry consists of mandatory and optional components.

3.2.1   Term (Mandatory)

The name of the business term, class definition, element, attribute, or acronym that is being defined.

Terms coming from the S-Series IPS specifications data models conform to the camel case naming convention of writing compound words or phrases such that each next word begins with a capital letter. The S-Series IPS specifications convention is to capitalize the first letter for class names (example: UpperCamelCase) and to use a lower case first letter for attribute names (example: lowerCamelCase). Refer to SX004G.

3.2.2   Definition (Mandatory)

A formal statement explaining the meaning or concept of a term. Definitions are intended to be definite, distinct, and clear.

The standard pattern for definitions in SX001G consists of the following parts:

- the term (word or phrase) to be defined
- the class of object or concept to which the term belongs
- the differentiating characteristics that distinguish it from all others of its class

Exceptions to this pattern are where the source of the definition comes from another specification that does not apply the same definition writing rules.

3.2.3   Type (Mandatory)

The type is a classification of the term into categories intended to provide context of the term to the reader.

The majority of the terms in SX001G are either Unified Modeling Language (UML) types or classes and attributes of the SX002D Common Data Model (CDM). Term types coming from the CDM will have the prefix "CDM", term types coming from UML will have the prefix "UML". Refer to SX004G for details on the CDM and UML types.

Types within the SX001G Glossary are:

- Acronym - a word formed from the initial letter or letters of each of the successive parts or major parts of a compound term
- Business Term
- CDM AuthorizedLife
- CDM ClassificationType
- CDM DateType
- CDM DescriptorType
- CDM exchange stereotype
- CDM IdentifierType
- CDM Organization
- CDM PropertyType
- CDM select stereotype
- CDM SerialNumberRange
- CDM Unit of Functionality
- UML Abstract class
- UML attributeGroup stereotype
- UML char
- UML Class
- UML compoundAttribute stereotype
- UML double
- UML extend stereotype

- UML int
- UML interface
- UML primitive stereotype
- UML relationship stereotype

Refer to SX004G for details on the CDM and UML types.

3.2.4 Reference (Optional)
Links to terms used within the definition of this term.

3.2.5 Note (Optional)
A note provides additional comments associated with the glossary term that are not part of the definition but can help convey the meaning or use of the term.

3.2.6 Example (Optional)
There can be examples of the term where such examples are necessary to describe the term.

3.2.7 Source of the definition (Optional)
Reference to a specification external to the S-Series specifications where the term is already defined, and the definition is reused in SX001G in part or in whole.

3.2.8 Formatting of classes and attributes
The names of attributes, classes and data types have a special formatting in the text for easier identification. Their formats are as follows:

- Classes and data types
- Attributes

Page intentionally blank.

Chapter 1.4

Maintenance of the specification

Table of contents
Page

List of tables

References

Table 1 References

Chap No./Document No.	Title
SX000i	International specification for Integrated Product Support (IPS)

1   Maintenance of the specification

SX001G is maintained by the Data Modeling and Exchange Working Group (DMEWG) operating under the supervision of the Integrated Logistics Support (ILS) Specifications Council. Both the DMEWG and the IPS Specifications Council include representatives from AeroSpace and Defense Industries Association of Europe (ASD) and Aerospace Industries Association of America (AIA) member companies and nations.

Issues related to SX001G can be raised using the change request tool found at www.sx000i.org. Change requests are submitted with the understanding that any revisions to SX001G can affect the other specifications in the S-Series IPS specifications, and that proposed changes are subject to international agreement among ASD and AIA member companies and nations.

Upon receipt of a change request, the DMEWG will follow the change management process described in SX000i, to gain consensus agreement from the participating organizations prior to the publication of changes. The DMEWG considers change proposals and ratifies them for incorporation into SX001G.

Page intentionally blank.

Applicable to: All

End of data module

Chapter 2

Glossary

Table of contents

Page intentionally blank.

Chapter 2.1

Glossary - A

Table of contents

List of tables

References

Table 1 References

Chap No./Document No.	Title
Chap 2.2	Glossary - B
Chap 2.3	Glossary - C
Chap 2.4	Glossary - D
Chap 2.5	Glossary - E
Chap 2.8	Glossary - H
Chap 2.9	Glossary - I
Chap 2.16	Glossary - P
Chap 2.19	Glossary - S
Chap 2.20	Glossary - T
Chap 2.21	Glossary - U

1   additionalAddressInformation

Definition

`additionalAddressInformation` is a description that provides additional information to further locate an address.

Examples

- First floor, apartment 7
- Building 7 in campus
- Suite 204

Type

- CDM DescriptorType

2   AdditionalTrainingNeed

Definition

`AdditionalTrainingNeed` is an <<attributeGroup>> that specifies additional learning required for the associated `CompetenceDefinitionItem` in order to qualify as the TaskPersonnelResource.

References

- `CompetenceDefinitionItem`, refer to Chap 2.3
- `TaskPersonnelResource`, refer to Chap 2.20

Type

- UML class

3   additionalTrainingNeedDescription

Definition

`additionalTrainingNeedDescription` is a description that gives more information on additional learning required.

Examples

- Experience
- Knowledge
- Skill
- Values
- Behavior

Type

- CDM `DescriptorType`

4   Aggregated Element UoF

Definition

The Aggregated Element UoF provides the capability to specify that an element within a breakdown represents a collection of elements for an identified purpose.

5   AggregatedElement

Definition

`AggregatedElement` is a `BreakdownElement` that is a container for a collection of BreakdownElements which are grouped for an identified purpose.

Reference

- `BreakdownElement`, refer to Chap 2.2

Type

- UML class

6   AggregatedElementRevision

Definition

`AggregatedElementRevision` is a `BreakdownElementRevision` representing an iteration applied to an `AggregatedElement`.

References

- `AggregatedElement`, refer to Para 5
- `BreakdownElementRevision`, refer to Chap 2.2

Type
- UML class

7   aggregatedElementType

Definition
`aggregatedElementType` is a classification that identifies further specialization for an `AggregatedElement`.

Reference
- `AggregatedElement`, refer to Para 5

Valid values
- FA (SX001G:familyBreakdownElement)
- FU (SX001G:functionBreakdownElement)
- SY (SX001G:systemBreakdownElement)
- GR (SX001G:groupBreakdownElement)

Type
- CDM ClassificationType

8   AIA

Definition
Aerospace Industries Association of America.

Type
- Acronym

9   AllocatedTaskLocation

Definition
`AllocatedTaskLocation` is a <<class>> that identifies where a `Task` is to be performed in the context of a given support solution.

Reference
- `Task`, refer to Chap 2.20

Type
- UML class

10   AllowedProductConfiguration

Definition
`AllowedProductConfiguration` is an <<extend>> interface that provides its associated data model to those classes that must define permitted combinations of hardware and software parts which can or must be installed in specific locations (positions).

Note 1
One and the same serialized product can adhere to different allowed product configurations over time.

Note 2
An allowed product configuration can also include associated engineering instructions that must be adhered to during assembly and operation and that demonstrates that a product complies with applicable regulations.

Example
– Applicable regulations may be a type certificate.

Type
– UML <<extend>> stereotype

11 AllowedProductConfigurationByConfigurationIdentifier

Definition
`AllowedProductConfigurationByConfigurationIdentifier` is a
<<class>> that defines an `AllowedProductConfiguration` by means other than a
part number.

Reference
– `AllowedProductConfiguration`, refer to <u>Para 10</u>

Type
– UML class

12 AllowedProductConfigurationHardwarePartAsDesigned

Definition
`AllowedProductConfigurationHardwarePartAsDesigned` is a
`HardwarePartAsDesigned` that is managed as an
`AllowedProductConfiguration`.

References
– `AllowedProductConfiguration`, refer to <u>Para 10</u>
– `HardwarePartAsDesigned`, refer to <u>Chap 2.8</u>

Type
– UML class

13 allowedProductConfigurationIdentifier

Definition
`allowedProductConfigurationIdentifier` is an identifier that establishes a
unique designator for an
`AllowedProductConfigurationByConfigurationIdentifier` and to
differentiate it from other instances of
`AllowedProductConfigurationByConfigurationIdentifier`.

References
– `AllowedProductConfigurationByConfigurationIdentifier`, refer
  to <u>Para 11</u>
– `identifier`, refer to <u>Chap 2.9</u>

Valid values
– ID (SX001G:allowedProductConfigurationIdentifier)

Type
– CDM `IdentifierType`

14 AllowedProductConfigurationItem

Definition
`AllowedProductConfigurationItem` is a <<select>> interface that identifies items which can be selected as an allowed product configuration.

Type
- UML <<select>> stereotype

15 AlternatePartAsDesigned

Definition
`AlternatePartAsDesigned` is a <<relationship>> that defines an alternate `PartAsDesigned` which can replace the base `PartAsDesigned` in all its usages ie, it is context independent, and is form, fit and function equivalent.

Note
A part can have one or more alternate parts. The alternate part is interchangeable with the base part in any/all uses.

Reference
- `PartAsDesigned`, refer to Chap 2.16

Type
- UML class

16 altitude

Definition
`altitude` is a string of characters that represents the height above or below a fixed reference point.

Reference
- height, refer to Chap 2.8

Example
- 34m above sea level

Type
- UML string

17 Analysis Candidate Item UoF

Definition
The Analysis Candidate Item UoF provides the capability to define decisions and results associated with support analysis activities.

18 AnalysisActivity

Definition
`AnalysisActivity` is a <<class>> that represents the objective for, and outcome of, an analysis carried out for the `AnalysisCandidateItem`.

Reference
- `AnalysisCandidateItem`, refer to Para 28

Type
- UML class

19   analysisActivityDecision

Definition

`analysisActivityDecision` is a classification that identifies if the `AnalysisActivity` is to be performed on the `AnalysisCandidateItem`.

References
- `AnalysisActivity`, refer to Para 18
- `AnalysisCandidateItem`, refer to Para 28

Valid values
- S (SX001G:selectedAnalysisActivity)
- R (SX001G:rejectedAnalysisActivity)
- O (SX001G:toBeDecidedAnalysisActivity)

Type
- CDM `ClassificationType`

20   analysisActivityDecisionRationale

Definition

`analysisActivityDecisionRationale` is a description that gives more information on the reason for the selection / non-selection of the `AnalysisActivity`.

Reference
- `AnalysisActivity`, refer to Para 18

Type
- CDM `DescriptorType`

21   AnalysisActivityRevision

Definition

`AnalysisActivityRevision` is a <<class>> representing an iteration applied to an `AnalysisActivity`.

Reference
- `AnalysisActivity`, refer to Para 18

Type
- UML class

22   analysisActivityRevisionDate

Definition

`analysisActivityRevisionDate` is a date that specifies when a `AnalysisActivityRevision` was defined.

Reference
- `AnalysisActivityRevision`, refer to Para 21

Type
- CDM `DateType`

23   analysisActivityRevisionIdentifier

Definition

`analysisActivityRevisionIdentifier` is an identifier that establishes a unique designator for an `AnalysisActivityRevision` and to differentiate it from other instances of `AnalysisActivityRevision`.

References
- `AnalysisActivityRevision`, refer to Para 21
- identifier, refer to Chap 2.9

Valid values
- ID (SX001G:analysisActivityRevisionIdentifier)

Type
- CDM `IdentifierType`

24   analysisActivityRevisionRationale

Definition

`analysisActivityRevisionRationale` is a description that gives more information on the justification for revising the defined `AnalysisActivity`.

Reference
- `AnalysisActivity`, refer to Para 18

Type
- CDM `DescriptorType`

25   analysisActivityRevisionStatus

Definition

`analysisActivityRevisionStatus` is a state that identifies the maturity of a `AnalysisActivityRevision`.

References
- `AnalysisActivityRevision`, refer to Para 21
- state, refer to Chap 2.19

Type
- CDM `StateType`

26   analysisActivityStatusDescription

Definition

`analysisActivityStatusDescription` is a description that gives further information on the progression of the `AnalysisActivity`.

Reference
- `AnalysisActivity`, refer to Para 18

Type
- CDM DescriptorType

27 analysisActivityType

Definition

`analysisActivityType` is a classification that identifies further specialization of `AnalysisActivity`.

Reference

- `AnalysisActivity`, refer to Para 18

Valid values

- CMP (SX001G:IsaComparativeAnalysis)
- HF (SX001G:IsaHumanFactorAnalysis)
- REL (SX001G:IsaReliabilityAnalysis)
- MNT (SX001G:IsaMaintainabilityAnalysis)
- TST (SX001G:IsaTestabilityAnalysis)
- FMA (SX001G:IsaFailureModeAndEffectAnalysis)
- COR (SX001G:IsaCorrectiveMaintenanceAnalysis)
- DMG (SX001G:IsaDamageAnalysis)
- SEV (SX001G:IsaSpecialEventAnalysis)
- LORA (SX001G:IsaLevelOfRepairAnalysis)
- MTA (SX001G:IsaMainenanceTaskAnalysis)
- SWL (SX001G:IsaSoftwareDataLoadingAnalysis)
- SWS (SX001G:IsaSoftwareSupportAnalysis)
- OP (SX001G:IsaOperationalAnalysis)
- SIM (SX001G:IsaSimulationOperationalScenariosAnalysis)
- TNA (SX001G:IsaTrainingNeedsAnalysis)
- OTH (SX001G:IsaOtherAnalysis)

Type

- CDM `ClassificationType`

28 AnalysisCandidateItem

Definition

`AnalysisCandidateItem` is an <<extend>> interface that provides its associated data model to those classes that can have an associated `AnalysisActivity`.

Reference

- `AnalysisActivity`, refer to Para 18

Type

- UML <<extend>> stereotype

29 AnalysisCandidateItemSelectionData

Definition

`AnalysisCandidateItemSelectionData` is an <<attributeGroup>> that summarizes decisions made for the `AnalysisCandidateItem` from a support analysis activities perspective.

Reference

- `AnalysisCandidateItem`, refer to Para 28

Type

- UML class

30 analysisCandidateItemSelectionIndicator

Definition

`analysisCandidateItemSelectionIndicator` is a classification that specifies to which extent analysis activities will be carried out on the associated `AnalysisCandidateItem`.

Reference
- `AnalysisCandidateItem`, refer to Para 28

Valid values
- F (SX001G:fullCandidateItem)
- P (SX001G:partialCandidateItem)
- N (SX001G:nonCandidateItem)
- O (SX001G:toBeDecidedCandidateItem)

Type
- CDM `ClassificationType`

31 analysisCandidateItemSelectionRationale

Definition

`analysisCandidateItemSelectionRationale` is a description that gives more information on the reason for the candidate selection.

Type
- CDM `DescriptorType`

32 Applicability Statement UoF

Definition

The Applicability Statement UoF provides the capability to define the situation or situations under which related items are valid.

33 ApplicabilityStatement

Definition

`ApplicabilityStatement` is a <<class>> that defines the situation or situations under which related items are valid.

Type
- UML class

34 applicabilityStatementDateRange

Definition

`applicabilityStatementDateRange` is a date range that defines the date interval for when the applicability evaluation can result in a TRUE result.

Note

If outside that date range, the `ApplicabilityStatement` always results in a FALSE statement.

Type
- CDM `DateRange`

35 applicabilityStatementDescription

Definition

`applicabilityStatementDescription` is a description that provides a human readable expression of the defined rule.

Type
- CDM `DescriptorType`

36 applicabilityStatementIdentifier

Definition

`applicabilityStatementIdentifier` is an identifier that establishes a unique designator for an `ApplicabilityStatement` and to differentiate it from other instances of `ApplicabilityStatement`.

References
- `ApplicabilityStatement`, refer to Para 33
- `identifier`, refer to Chap 2.9

Valid values
- ID (SX001G:applicabilityStatementIdentifier)

Type
- CDM `IdentifierType`

37 ApplicabilityStatementItem

Definition

`ApplicabilityStatementItem` is an <<extend>> interface that provides its associated data model to those classes which can have restricted validity as defined by an associated `ApplicabilityStatement`.

Reference
- `ApplicabilityStatement`, refer to Para 33

Type
- UML <<extend>> stereotype

38 ApplicableDecisionTreeTemplate

Definition

`ApplicableDecisionTreeTemplate` is a <<relationship>> that identifies a `DecisionTreeTemplate` which can be used for the `DecisionTreeAnalysisItem`.

References
- `DecisionTreeAnalysisItem`, refer to Chap 2.4
- `DecisionTreeTemplate`, refer to Chap 2.4

Type
- UML class

39 applicableSerialNumberRange

Definition

`applicableSerialNumberRange` is a serial number range that identifies a limited effectivity with respect to a given interval of serialized items.

Type
- CDM `SerialNumberRange`

40 ASD

Definition

Aerospace and Defence Industries Association of Europe

Type
- Acronym

41 assembly

Definition

`assembly` is a string of characters that represents the unit or assembly attribute of the data module code.

Reference
- `unit`, refer to Chap 2.21

Type
- UML string

42 AssociatedEnvironmentDefinition

Definition

`AssociatedEnvironmentDefinition` is a <<relationship>> that associates an `EnvironmentDefinitionItem` with an `EnvironmentDefinition` relevant to its existence, operation and/or support.

References
- `EnvironmentDefinition`, refer to Chap 2.5
- `EnvironmentDefinitionItem`, refer to Chap 2.5

Type
- UML class

43 AuthorityDrivenTaskRequirement

Definition

`AuthorityDrivenTaskRequirement` is an <<attributeGroup>> that collects information on task requirement derived from regulations and/or other authoritative sources.

Type
UML class

44 AuthorityToOperate

Definition

`AuthorityToOperate` is a <<class>> that represents a certification allowing a specific configuration of a product to be put into operation.

Note 1

A design change cannot be put into operation without re-certification.

Note 2

Type certificate for an aircraft signifies the airworthiness of its design.

Type

– UML class

45 authorityToOperateIdentifier

Definition

authorityToOperateIdentifier is an identifier that establishes a unique designator for an AuthorityToOperate and to differentiate it from other instances of AuthorityToOperate.

References

– AuthorityToOperate, refer to Para 44
– identifier, refer to Chap 2.9

Valid values

– ID (SX001G:authorityToOperateIdentifier)

Type

– CDM IdentifierType

46 AuthorizedLife

Definition

AuthorizedLife is a <<compoundAttribute>> that identifies the maximum usage limit and upon reaching this limit any further usage of the item must be re-authorized.

Type

– UML class

47 authorizedLifeValue

Definition

authorizedLifeValue is a property that specifies the maximum usage limit.

Type

– CDM PropertyType

Page intentionally blank.

Chapter 2.2

Glossary - B

Table of contents

List of tables

References

Table 1 References

Chap No./Document No.	Title
Chap 2.9	Glossary - I
Chap 2.16	Glossary - P
Chap 2.19	Glossary - S
Chap 2.26	Glossary - Z

1 BaseObject

Definition

BaseObject is a <<class>> that represents the most elementary behavior that is common to all S-Series classes.

Type
- UML class

2 BatchHardwarePart

Definition

BatchHardwarePart is <<class>> that represent actual physical parts which can be identified by its lot membership.

Type
- UML class

3 batchPartIdentifier

Definition

batchPartIdentifier is an identifier that establishes a unique designator for a batch of actual parts and to differentiate it from other batches.

Reference
- identifier, refer to Chap 2.9

Valid values
- ID (SX001G:batchPartIdentifier)

Type
- CDM IdentifierType

4 Breakdown

Definition

Breakdown is a <<class>> that identifies a specific partitioning of a Product to form a parent-child structure of related instances of BreakdownElement.

References
- BreakdownElement, refer to Para 6
- Product, refer to Chap 2.16

Type
- UML class

5 Breakdown Structure UoF

Definition
The Breakdown Structure UoF provides the capability to define any number of hierarchical structures for a specific Product or Product variant.

References
- Breakdown, refer to Para 4
- Product, refer to Chap 2.16

6 BreakdownElement

Definition
BreakdownElement is a <<class>> defining a partition of a Product that is used in one or many instances of Breakdown.

References
- Breakdown, refer to Para 4
- Product, refer to Chap 2.16

Type
- UML class

7 breakdownElementChildSequenceNumber

Definition
breakdownElementChildSequenceNumber is a string of characters that controls the order for the included child element.

Note
The sequence number can be used to control how child elements are presented in eg, a list.

Type
- UML string

8 breakdownElementDescription

Definition
breakdownElementDescription is a description that gives more information on the BreakdownElement.

Reference
- BreakdownElement, refer to Para 6

Type
- CDM DescriptorType

9 breakdownElementEssentiality

Definition
breakdownElementEssentiality is a classification that identifies the operational importance of the BreakdownElement at the Product level.

Note
Based on the criticality as defined during the FMECA.

References
- `BreakdownElement`, refer to Para 6
- `Product`, refer to Chap 2.16

Valid values
- 3 (SX001G:nonCriticalBreakdownElement)
- 2 (SX001G:partialCriticalBreakdownElement)
- 1 (SX001G:criticalBreakdownElement)

Type
- CDM `ClassificationType`

10 breakdownElementIdentifier

Definition
`breakdownElementIdentifier` is an identifier that establishes a unique designator for a `BreakdownElement` and to differentiate it from other instances of `BreakdownElement`.

Note
Can be used to establish a hierarchical structure of the technical system.

References
- `BreakdownElement`, refer to Para 6
- `identifier`, refer to Chap 2.9

Valid values
- ID (SX001G:breakdownElementIdentifier)
- SNS (SX001G:standardNumberingSystemIdentifier)
- LCN (SX001G:fullLogisticsSupportAnalysisControlNumber)
- CSN (SX001G:figureItemIdentifier)
- ASD (SX001G:asdSystemHardwareIdentificationCode)

Examples
- The Standard Numbering System defined by S1000D.
- The combination of logistics support analysis control number and alternate logistics support analysis control number within GEIA-STD-0007.

Type
- CDM `IdentifierType`

11 BreakdownElementInZone

Definition
`BreakdownElementInZone` is a <<relationship>> where a `BreakdownElementInZoneItem` relates to the `ZoneElement` where it is located.

References
- `BreakdownElementInZoneItem`, refer to Para 12
- `ZoneElement`, refer to Chap 2.26

Type
- UML class

12   BreakdownElementInZoneItem

Definition

`BreakdownElementInZoneItem` is an <<extend>> interface that provides its associated data model to those classes that implement it.

Type
- UML <<extend>> stereotype

13   breakdownElementName

Definition

`breakdownElementName` is a name by which the `BreakdownElement` is known and can be easily referenced.

Reference
- `BreakdownElement`, refer to Para 6

Type
- CDM `NameType`

14   BreakdownElementRevision

Definition

`BreakdownElementRevision` is a <<class>> representing an iteration applied to a `BreakdownElement`.

Reference
- `BreakdownElement`, refer to Para 6

Type
- UML class

15   breakdownElementRevisionDate

Definition

`breakdownElementRevisionDate` is a date that specifies when the `BreakdownElement` was revised.

Reference
- `BreakdownElement`, refer to Para 6

Type
- CDM `DateType`

16   breakdownElementRevisionIdentifier

Definition

`breakdownElementRevisionIdentifier` is an identifier that establishes a unique designator for a `BreakdownElementRevision` and to differentiate it from other instances of `BreakdownElementRevision`.

References
- `BreakdownElementRevision`, refer to Para 14
- `identifier`, refer to Chap 2.9

Valid values
- ID (SX001G:breakdownElementRevisionIdentifier)

Type
- CDM `IdentifierType`

17 breakdownElementRevisionRationale

Definition
`breakdownElementRevisionRationale` is a description that gives more information on the justification for revising the `BreakdownElement`.

Reference
- `BreakdownElement`, refer to Para 6

Type
- CDM `DescriptorType`

18 BreakdownElementRevisionRelationship

Definition
`BreakdownElementRevisionRelationship` is a <<relationship>> where one `BreakdownElementRevision` relates to another `BreakdownElement` or `BreakdownElementRevision`.

References
- `BreakdownElement`, refer to Para 6
- `BreakdownElementRevision`, refer to Para 14

Type
- UML class

19 BreakdownElementRevisionRelationshipItem

Definition
`BreakdownElementRevisionRelationshipItem` is a <<select>> interface that provides the capability to be associated with a `BreakdownElementRevision`.

Reference
- `BreakdownElementRevision`, refer to Para 14

Type
- UML <<select>> stereotype

20 breakdownElementRevisionRelationshipType

Definition
`breakdownElementRevisionRelationshipType` is a classification that identifies the meaning of the established relationship.

Note
The related breakdown elements do not need to be used in the same breakdown, ie, it can be used to establish the relationship between a breakdown element in a functional breakdown and a breakdown element in a physical breakdown.

Valid values
- AP (SX001G:breakdownElementAccessPoint)

- FUPH (SX001G:functionalToPhysicalBreakdownElementRelationship)
- ALT (SX001G:alternateToBreakdownElement)

Type
- CDM `ClassificationType`

21 breakdownElementRevisionStatus

Definition
`breakdownElementRevisionStatus` is a state that identifies the maturity of a
`BreakdownElementRevision`.

References
- `BreakdownElementRevision`, refer to Para 14
- state, refer to Chap 2.19

Type
- CDM `StateType`

22 BreakdownElementStructure

Definition
BreakdownElementStructure is a <<relationship>> that establishes a hierarchical structure
between two usages of BreakdownElement that belong to the same BreakdownRevision.

References
- `BreakdownElement`, refer to Para 6
- `BreakdownRevision`, refer to Para 29

Type
- UML class

23 breakdownElementUsageIdentifier

Definition
`breakdownElementUsageIdentifier` is an identifier that establishes a unique
designator for a `BreakdownElementUsageInBreakdown` and to differentiate it from
other instances of `BreakdownElementUsageInBreakdown`.

References
- `BreakdownElementUsageInBreakdown`, refer to Para 24
- identifier, refer to Chap 2.9

Valid values
- ID (SX001G:breakdownElementUsageIdentifier)

Type
- CDM `IdentifierType`

24 BreakdownElementUsageInBreakdown

Definition
`BreakdownElementUsageInBreakdown` is a <<class>> that represents a member
of a `BreakdownRevision`.

Note

A `BreakdownElementRevision` can belong to multiple `BreakdownRevisions`.

Reference

- `BreakdownRevision`, refer to Para 29

Type

- UML class

25   breakdownElementUsageQuantity

Definition

`breakdownElementUsageQuantity` is a property that specifies the amount of the `BreakdownElement` used in its parent `BreakdownElement`.

Note

If no value is given, it must be interpreted as value "1" with a unit of "each". For as required amounts, the text property is used with "As Required" or other text as appropriate.

Reference

- `BreakdownElement`, refer to Para 6

Type

- CDM `PropertyType`

26   BreakdownElementUsageRelationship

Definition

`BreakdownElementUsageRelationship` is a <<relationship>> where one usage of a `BreakdownElement` relates to the usage of another `BreakdownElement`.

Note

Both related instances of `BreakdownElementUsageInBreakdown` must reside within the same `BreakdownRevision`.

Reference

- `BreakdownElement`, refer to Para 6

Example

- Version C of a radio is restricted to the use of software version B in breakdown revision 2.

Type

- UML class

27   breakdownElementUsageRelationshipType

Definition

`breakdownElementUsageRelationshipType` is a classification that identifies the meaning of the established relationship.

Valid values

- AND (SX001G:mutualBreakdownElementInclusion)
- XOR (SX001G:mutualBreakdownElementExclusion)

Type

- CDM `ClassificationType`

28   BreakdownItem

Definition

BreakdownItem is an <<extend>> interface that provides its associated data model to those classes that implement it.

Type

- UML <<extend>> stereotype

29   BreakdownRevision

Definition

BreakdownRevision is a <<class>> representing an iteration applied to a Breakdown.

Note

BreakdownRevision is used to document design iterations and not breakdown variants.

Reference

- Breakdown, refer to Para 4

Type

- UML class

30   breakdownRevisionDate

Definition

breakdownRevisionDate is a date that specifies when the Breakdown was revised.

Reference

- Breakdown, refer to Para 4

Type

- CDM DateType

31   breakdownRevisionIdentifier

Definition

breakdownRevisionIdentifier is an identifier that establishes a unique designator for a BreakdownRevision and to differentiate it from other instances of BreakdownRevision.

References

- BreakdownRevision, refer to Para 29
- identifier, refer to Chap 2.9

Valid values

- ID (SX001G:breakdownRevisionIdentifier)

Type

- CDM IdentifierType

32   breakdownRevisionRationale

Definition

breakdownRevisionRationale is a description that gives more information on the justification for revising the Breakdown.

Reference
- Breakdown, refer to Para 4

Type
- CDM DescriptorType

33 BreakdownRevisionRelationship

Definition
BreakdownRevisionRelationship is a <<relationship>> where one BreakdownRevision relates to another BreakdownRevision.

Reference
- BreakdownRevision, refer to Para 29

Type
- UML class

34 breakdownRevisionRelationshipType

Definition
breakdownRevisionRelationshipType is a classification that identifies the meaning of the established relationship.

Valid values
- BO (SX001G:basedOnBreakdownRevision)
- M (SX001G:matchesBreakdownRevision)

Type
- CDM ClassificationType

35 breakdownRevisionStatus

Definition
breakdownRevisionStatus is a state that identifies the maturity of a BreakdownRevision.

References
- BreakdownRevision, refer to Para 29
- state, refer to Chap 2.19

Type
- CDM StateType

36 breakdownType

Definition
breakdownType is a classification that identifies the perspective from which the Breakdown is defined.

Reference
- Breakdown, refer to Para 4

Valid values
- PH (SX001G:physicalBreakdown)
- PR (SX001G:provisioningBreakdown)
- ASD (SX001G:asdSystemHardwareBreakdown)

- FU (SX001G:functionalBreakdown)
- SY (SX001G:systemBreakdown)
- FAM (SX001G:familyBreakdown)
- ZONE (SX001G:zonalBreakdown)
- HY (SX001G:hybridBreakdown)

Type

- CDM ClassificationType

Page intentionally blank.

Chapter 2.3

Glossary - C

Table of contents

Page

List of tables

References

Table 1 References

Chap No./Document No.	Title
Chap 2.5	Glossary - E
Chap 2.8	Glossary - H
Chap 2.9	Glossary - I
Chap 2.16	Glossary - P
Chap 2.19	Glossary - S
Chap 2.21	Glossary - U
Chap 2.22	Glossary - V

1   CDM

Definition
Common Data Model

Type
–   Acronym

2   Capability Definition UoF

Definition
The Capability Definition UoF provides the possibility to define functional and physical abilities enabled by the associated item.

3   CapabilityDefinition

Definition
CapabilityDefinition is a <<class>> that defines an ability.

Examples
–   Small-sized ammunition resistance
–   Air vehicle accommodation
–   1 month autonomy
–   Body detection
–   Unpaved runway landing
–   Paratroop launch
–   Patient transport
–   Air-to-air refuel

- Deep water exploration

Type
- UML class

4   capabilityDefinitionCategory

Definition
capabilityDefinitionCategory is a classification that identifies a generalization that organizes capabilities into an overarching capability taxonomy.

Valid values
- OP (SX001G:operationalCapability)
- SU (SX001G:supportCapability)
- MI (SX001G:MissionCapability)

Type
- CDM ClassificationType

5   CapabilityDefinitionCharacteristic

Definition
CapabilityDefinitionCharacteristic is a <<class> that specifies a measurable or observable feature which is significant for the CapabilityDefinition.

Reference
- CapabilityDefinition, refer to Para 3

Example
- Provide pressure air up to 100 psi

Type
- UML class

6   capabilityDefinitionCharacteristicDescription

Definition
capabilityDefinitionCharacteristicDescription is a description that gives more information on the CapabilityDefinitionCharacteristic.

Reference
- CapabilityDefinitionCharacteristic, refer to Para 5

Type
- CDM DescriptorType

7   capabilityDefinitionCharacteristicName

Definition
capabilityDefinitionCharacteristicName is a name by which the CapabilityDefinitionCharacteristic is known and can be easily referenced.

Reference
- CapabilityDefinitionCharacteristic, refer to Para 5

Type
- CDM NameType

8   capabilityDefinitionCharacteristicValue

Definition

`capabilityDefinitionCharacteristicValue` is a property that represents a measurable or observable characteristic for that is significant to the `CapabilityDefinition`.

Reference

- `CapabilityDefinition`, refer to <u>Para 3</u>

Type

- CDM `PropertyType`

9   capabilityDefinitionCharacteristicValueComparisonOperator

Definition

`capabilityDefinitionCharacteristicValueComparisonOperatorr` is a classification that identifies the comparison operator which is to be used in order to qualify whether an actual capability complies with the defined `CapabilityDefinition`.

Reference

- `CapabilityDefinition`, refer to <u>Para 3</u>

Type

- CDM `ClassificationType`

10   capabilityDefinitionDescription

Definition

`capabilityDefinitionDescription` is a description that gives more information on the defined capability.

Type

- CDM `DescriptorType`

11   capabilityDefinitionIdentifier

Definition

`capabilityDefinitionIdentifier` is an identifier that establishes a unique designator for a `CapabilityDefinition` and to differentiate it from other instances of `CapabilityDefinition`.

References

- `CapabilityDefinition`, refer to <u>Para 3</u>
- `identifier`, refer to <u>Chap 2.9</u>

Valid values

- ID (SX001G:capabilityDefinitionIdentifier)

Type

- CDM `IdentifierType`

12   CapabilityDefinitionItem

Definition

`CapabilityDefinitionItem` is an <<extend>> interface that provides its associated data model to those classes that can have an associated `CapabilityDefinition`.

Reference
CapabilityDefinition, refer to Para 3

Type
– UML <<extend>> stereotype

13 capabilityDefinitionName

Definition
capabilityDefinitionName is a name by which the CapabilityDefinition is known and can be easily referenced.

Reference
– CapabilityDefinition, refer to Para 3

Type
– CDM NameType

14 CapabilityDefinitionRevision

Definition
CapabilityDefinitionRevision is a <<class>> representing an iteration applied to a CapabilityDefinition.

Reference
– CapabilityDefinition, refer to Para 3

Type
UML class

15 capabilityDefinitionRevisionDate

Definition
capabilityDefinitionRevisionDate is a date that specifies when the CapabilityDefinition was revised.

Reference
– CapabilityDefinition, refer to Para 3

Type
– CDM DateType

16 capabilityDefinitionRevisionIdentifier

Definition
capabilityDefinitionRevisionIdentifier is an identifier that establishes a unique designator for a CapabilityDefinitionRevision and to differentiate it from other instances of CapabilityDefinitionRevision.

References
– CapabilityDefinitionRevision, refer to Para 14
– identifier, refer to Chap 2.9

Valid values
– ID (SX001G:capabilityDefinitionRevisionIdentifier)

Type
- CDM IdentifierType

17 capabilityDefinitionRevisionRationale

Definition
capabilityDefinitionRevisionRationale is a description that provides a justification for revising the CapabilityDefinition.

Reference
- CapabilityDefinition, refer to Para 3

Type
- CDM DescriptorType

18 capabilityDefinitionRevisionStatus

Definition
capabilityDefinitionRevisionStatus is a state that identifies the maturity of an CapabilityDefinitionRevision.

References
- CapabilityDefinitionRevision, refer to Para 14
- state, refer to Chap 2.19

Type
- CDM StateType

19 Change Information UoF

Definition
The Change Information UoF provides the capability to identify that an item has been affected by a change authorization.

20 ChangeAuthorization

Definition
ChangeAuthorization is a <<class>> that is the record of the permission to modify product design, its procedures and/or associated product support data.

Type
- UML class

21 changeAuthorizationIdentifier

Definition
changeAuthorizationIdentifier is an identifier that establishes a unique designator for an ChangeAuthorization and to differentiate it from other instances of ChangeAuthorization

References
- ChangeAuthorization, refer to Para 20
- identifier, refer to Chap 2.9

Valid values
- ID (SX001G:changeAuthorizationIdentifier)
- AMN (SX001G:changeAmendmentNumber)

– CAN (SX001G:changeAuthorizationNumber)

Type
– CDM `IdentifierType`

22 ChangeControlledItem

Definition
`ChangeControlledItem` is an <<extend>> interface that provides its associated data model to those classes that can be affected by a `ChangeAuthorization`.

Reference
– `ChangeAuthorization`, refer to <u>Para 20</u>

Type
– UML <<extend>> stereotype

23 ChangeNotification

Definition
`ChangeNotification` is a <<relationship>> that identifies an item changed due to the associated `ChangeAuthorization`.

Reference
– `ChangeAuthorization`, refer to <u>Para 20</u>

Type
– UML class

24 changeNotificationDescription

Definition
`changeNotificationDescription` is a description providing a summary of affects made to the related item due to a `ChangeAuthorization`.

Reference
– `ChangeAuthorization`, refer to <u>Para 20</u>

Type
– CDM `DescriptorType`

25 changeNotificationType

Definition
`changeNotificationType` is a classification that identifies a change effect as belonging to a group of change effects sharing a particular characteristic or set of characteristics.

Valid values
– T (SX001G:technicalChangeNotification)
– A (SX001G:applicabilityChangeNotification)
– E (SX001G:editorialChangeNotification)
– M (SX001G:markupChangeNotification)

Type
– CDM `ClassificationType`

26   ChangeRequest

Definition

`ChangeRequest` is a <<class>> that represents a formal proposal for a modification to a configuration item upon a given baseline.

Note

Typical configuration items are eg, `Product`, `PartAsDesigned`, and `BreakdownElement`.

Type

– UML class

27   changeRequestDescription

Definition

`changeRequestDescription` is a description, providing detailed explanation of the desired change.

Type

– CDM `DescriptorType`

28   changeRequestIdentifier

Definition

`changeRequestIdentifier` is an identifier that establishes a unique designator for a `ChangeRequest` and to differentiate it from other instances of `ChangeRequest`.

References

– `ChangeRequest`, refer to Para 26
– identifier, refer to Chap 2.9

Valid values

– ID (SX001G:changeRequestIdentifier)

Type

– CDM `IdentifierType`

29   changeRequestIntendedEffect

Definition

`changeRequestIntendedEffect` is a description, providing detailed explanation of the expected effect of the change.

Type

– CDM `DescriptorType`

30   ChangeRequestRationale

Definition

`ChangeRequestRationale` is a <<relationship>> that associates a `ChangeRequest` with a `ChangeRequestRationaleItem`.

References

– `ChangeRequest`, refer to Para 26
– `ChangeRequestRationaleItem`, refer to Para 31

Type
- UML class

31   ChangeRequestRationaleItem

Definition
ChangeRequestRationaleItem is a <<select>> interface that identifies analysis items which can support a ChangeRequest.

Reference
- ChangeRequest, refer to Para 26

Type
- UML <<select>> stereotype

32   changeRequestStatus

Definition
changeRequestStatus is a state, that documents the progress of the ChangeRequest within its lifecycle.

References
- ChangeRequest, refer to Para 26
- state, refer to Chap 2.19

Valid values
- IW (SX001G:inWorkChangeRequest)
- A (SX001G:approvedChangeRequest)
- R (SX001G:rejectedChangeRequest)
- S (SX001G:submittedChangeRequest)

Type
- CDM StateType

33   ChangeRequestTarget

Definition
ChangeRequestTarget is a <<relationship>> that associates a ChangeRequest with a ChangeRequestTargetItem.

References
- ChangeRequest, refer to Para 26
- ChangeRequestTargetItem, refer to Para 34

Type
- UML class

34   ChangeRequestTargetItem

Definition
ChangeRequestTargetItem is a <<select>> interface that identifies items which can be the subject for a ChangeRequest.

Reference
- ChangeRequest, refer to Para 26

Type
- UML <<select>> stereotype

35   Circuit Breaker UoF

Definition
The Circuit Breaker UoF provides the capability to define circuit breakers and their locations.

36   CircuitBreaker

Definition
CircuitBreaker is a <<class>> that represents an individual circuit breaker identified in the context of a defined Product.

Reference
- Product, refer to Chap 2.16

Type
- UML class

37   circuitBreakerIdentifier

Definition
circuitBreakerIdentifier is an identifier that establishes a unique designator for a CircuitBreaker and to differentiate it from other instances of CircuitBreaker.

References
- CircuitBreaker, refer to Para 36
- identifier, refer to Chap 2.9

Valid values
- ID (SX001G:circuitBreakerIdentifier)

Type
- CDM IdentifierType

38   CircuitBreakerLocation

Definition
CircuitBreakerLocation is a <<relationship>> that identifies the item on which the CircuitBreaker is placed.

Reference
- CircuitBreaker, refer to Para 36

Type
- UML class

39   circuitBreakerLocationDescription

Definition
circuitBreakerLocationDescription is a description that provides further details on where the CircuitBreaker is located on the referenced CircuitBreakerLocationItem.

References
- CircuitBreaker, refer to Para 36

- `CircuitBreakerLocationItem`, refer to Para 40

Type
- CDM `DescriptorType`

40 CircuitBreakerLocationItem

Definition

`CircuitBreakerLocationItem` is a <<select>> interface that identifies items which can be selected in order to determine the location for a circuit breaker.

Type
- UML <<select>> stereotype

41 circuitBreakerName

Definition

`circuitBreakerName` is a name by which the `CircuitBreaker` is known and can be easily referenced

Reference
- `CircuitBreaker`, refer to Para 36

Type
- CDM `NameType`

42 CircuitBreakerSetting

Definition

`CircuitBreakerSetting` is a <<class>> that specifies an individual circuit breaker that must be in a specific state.

Reference
- `state`, refer to Chap 2.19

Type
- UML class

43 circuitBreakerSettingIdentifier

Definition

`circuitBreakerSettingIdentifier` is an identifier that establishes a unique designator for a defined circuit breaker setting, and to differentiate it from other instances of circuit breaker setting.

Reference
- `identifier`, refer to Chap 2.9

Valid values
- ID (SX001G:circuitBreakerSettingIdentifier)

Type
- CDM `IdentifierType`

44 CircuitBreakerSettings

Definition

`CircuitBreakerSettings` is a <<class>> that identifies a set of circuit breakers that must be set in specific states.

Type

- UML class

45 circuitBreakerSettingsIdentifier

Definition

`circuitBreakerSettingsIdentifier` is an identifier that establishes a unique designator for a defined set of circuit breaker settings, and to differentiate it from other instances of circuit breaker settings.

Reference

- `identifier`, refer to Chap 2.9

Valid values

- ID (SX001G:circuitBreakerSettingsIdentifier)

Type

- CDM `IdentifierType`

46 circuitBreakerSettingsOrdered

Definition

`circuitBreakerSettingsOrdered` is a Boolean that defines if the individual circuit breaker setting must be performed in the specified order.

Note 1

True specifies that the circuit breaker settings must be accomplished in the defined order.

Note 2

False specifies that the circuit breaker settings can be accomplished in any order.

Type

- UML `Boolean`

47 circuitBreakerState

Definition

`circuitBreakerState` is a state that identifies the position that a given circuit breaker must be in after the accomplishment of a defined circuit breaker setting.

Reference

- `state`, refer to Chap 2.19

Valid values

- VC (SX001G:verifyCloseCircuitBreakerState)
- VO (SX001G:verifyOpenCircuitBreakerState)
- C (SX001G:closedCircuitBreakerState)
- O (SX001G:openedCircuitBreakerState)

Type

- CDM `StateType`

48 circuitBreakerType

Definition

circuitBreakerType is a classification that defines the technical principle for the CircuitBreaker.

Reference

- CircuitBreaker, refer to Para 36

Valid values

- ELMEC (SX001G:electroMechanicCircuitBreaker)
- CLIP (SX001G:dummyCircuitBreaker)
- ELTRO (SX001G:electronicCircuitBreaker)

Type

- CDM ClassificationType

49 cityName

Definition

cityName is a name by which an incorporated municipal unit is known and can be easily referenced.

Reference

- unit, refer to Chap 2.21

Type

- CDM NameType

50 classificationDate

Definition

classificationDate is a calendar date that identifies when the classification was recorded.

Type

- CDM DateType

51 classificationDateTime

Definition

classificationDateTime is a calendar date and time that identifies when the classification was recorded.

Type

- CDM DateTimeType

52 ClassificationType

Definition

ClassificationType is an S-Series IPS specifications defined <<primitive>> that represents a finite set of values which are used to characterize the associated information for a defined purpose.

Note

Each term used for classification, and defined within the S-Series ILS specifications, has a definition in SX001G.

Type
- UML class

53 classifier

Definition

`classifier` is a word or code that represents the term used for classification.

Type
- CDM `validValue`

54 ClassInstanceAssertItem

Definition

`ClassInstanceAssertItem` is a <<select>> interface that identifies classes from which an instance can be used as the `EvaluationByAssertionOfClassInstance` assert item.

Reference
- `EvaluationByAssertionOfClassInstance`, refer to Chap 2.5

Type
- UML <<select>> stereotype

55 Competence Definition UoF

Definition

The Competence Definition UoF supports the definition of abilities, craft, profession, and proficiency.

56 CompetenceDefinitionItem

Definition

`CompetenceDefinitionItem` is a <<select>> interface that identifies items which define measurable or observable possession of knowledge and skills.

Type
- UML <<select>> stereotype

57 ConditionDefinitionItem

Definition

`ConditionDefinitionItem` is a <<select>> interface that identifies classes from which an instance can be used as the `EvaluationByAssertionOfCondition` assert condition.

Reference
- `EvaluationByAssertionOfCondition`, refer to Chap 2.5

Type
- UML <<select>> stereotype

58 ConditionInstance

Definition

`ConditionInstance` is a <<class>> that defines an individual concept or object having the characteristics of a generic `ConditionType`.

Reference
- `ConditionType`, refer to Para 62

Example
- Uniquely identified service bulletin

Type
- UML class

59 conditionInstanceDescription

Definition
`conditionInstanceDescription` is a description that gives more information on the meaning of the `ConditionInstance`.

Reference
- `ConditionInstance`, refer to Para 58

Type
- CDM `DescriptorType`

60 conditionInstanceIdentifier

Definition
`conditionInstanceIdentifier` is an identifier that establishes a unique designator for a `ConditionInstance` and to differentiate it from other instances of `ConditionInstance`.

References
- `ConditionInstance`, refer to Para 58
- `identifier`, refer to Chap 2.9

Valid values
- ID (SX001G:conditionInstanceIdentifier)
- SB (SX001G:serviceBulletinIdentifier)

Type
- CDM `IdentifierType`

61 conditionInstanceName

Definition
`conditionInstanceName` is a name by which the `ConditionInstance` is known and can be easily referenced.

Reference
- `ConditionInstance`, refer to Para 58

Type
- CDM `NameType`

62 ConditionType

Definition
`ConditionType` is a <<class>> that defines a concept or an object that needs to be included in applicability statements where the concept or object is not already represented in the data model.

Example
- Environmental conditions

Type
- UML class

63 ConditionTypeAssertMember

Definition
ConditionTypeAssertMember is <<class>> that defines a member for a given
ConditionType which can be mapped to a Boolean expression and be evaluated to be either
TRUE or FALSE.

Reference
- ConditionType, refer to Para 62

Type
- UML class

64 conditionTypeAssertMemberAssertValue

Definition
conditionTypeAssertMemberAssertValue is a numerical property that specifies
values which can be used to further characterize the ConditionTypeAssertMember.

Reference
ConditionTypeAssertMember, refer to Para 63

Type
CDM PropertyType

65 conditionTypeAssertMemberAssertValueComparisonOperator

Definition
conditionTypeAssertMemberAssertValueComparisonOperator is a
classification that identifies a mathematical operation to be applied when testing a value against
a defined conditionTypeAssertMemberAssertValue.

References
- conditionTypeAssertMemberAssertValue, refer to Para 64
- value, refer to Chap 2.22

Examples
- Greater than
- Less than

Type
- CDM ClassificationType

66 conditionTypeAssertMemberDescription

Definition
conditionTypeAssertMemberDescription is a description that gives more
information on meaning of the condition type assert member.

Type
- CDM DescriptorType

67   conditionTypeAssertMemberName

Definition

`conditionTypeAssertMemberName` is a name that identifies a condition type member assert value.

Reference

– `value`, refer to Chap 2.22

Type

– CDM `NameType`

68   conditionTypeDescription

Definition

`conditionTypeDescription` is a description that gives more information on the meaning of the condition type.

Type

– CDM `DescriptorType`

69   conditionTypeName

Definition

`conditionTypeName` is a name by which the ConditionType is known and can be easily referenced.

Reference

– `ConditionType`, refer to Para 62

Examples

– Service bulletin
– Ashore or afloat
– Operational environment
– Maintenance environment

Type

– CDM `NameType`

70   configurationConformanceEndDateTime

Definition

`configurationConformanceEndDateTime` is a date and time that specifies the point in time when the `SerializedProductVariant` no longer complies with the associated product configuration.

Reference

– `SerializedProductVariant`, refer to Chap 2.19

Type

– CDM `DateTimeType`

71   configurationConformanceStartDateTime

Definition
`configurationConformanceStartDateTime` is a date and time that specifies the point in time when the `SerializedProductVariant` changed to the associated product configuration.

Reference
`SerializedProductVariant`, refer to Chap 2.19

Type
-   CDM `DateTimeType`

72   Concession

Definition
Concession is an authorization granted before execution to depart from a particular performance of the contract, specification or reference document.

Note
Concession may be limited to a specific number of units or a specific period of time

Type
-   Business Term

73   ContainedSubstance

Definition
`ContainedSubstance` is a <<relationship>> that associates a `HardwarePartAsDesigned` with a contained `SubstanceDefinition`.

References
-   `HardwarePartAsDesigned`, refer to Chap 2.8
-   `SubstanceDefinition`, refer to Chap 2.19

Type
-   UML class

74   Contract

Definition
`Contract` is a <<class>> that represents a binding agreement between two or more parties.

Examples
-   Subcontract
-   Leasing contract
-   Procurement contract
-   Service contract

Type
-   UML class

75   contractIdentifier

Definition
`contractIdentifier` is an identifier that establishes a unique designator for a Contract and to differentiate it from other instances of `Contract`.

Reference
- Contract, refer to Para 73

Valid values
- ID (SX001G:contractIdentifier)

Type
- CDM IdentifierType

76   ContractItem

Definition
ContractItem is a <<select>> interface that identifies items which can be selected for the Contract.

Reference
- Contract, refer to Para 73

Type
- UML <<select>> stereotype

77   ContractItemDetails

Definition
ContractItemDetails is a <<relationship>> that identifies an item which is the subject of the Contract.

Reference
- Contract, refer to Para 73

Type
- UML class

78   contractItemDetailsContractQuantity

Definition
contractItemDetailsContractQuantity is a property that identifies the number of contract items that are included in the Contract

Reference
- Contract, refer to Para 73

Type
- CDM PropertyType

79   contractName

Definition
contractName is a name by which the Contract is known and can be easily referenced.

Reference
- Contract, refer to Para 73

Type
- CDM NameType

80   ContractParty

Definition

ContractParty is a <<relationship>> that identifies a Contract stakeholder.

Reference

- Contract, refer to Para 73

Type
- UML class

81   contractPartyRole

Definition

contractPartyRole is a classification that defines the purpose of the association between a ContractParty and the Contract.

References
- Contract, refer to Para 73
- ContractParty, refer to Para 80

Valid values
- CTR (SX001G:contractor)
- USER (SX001G:user)
- CUS (SX001G:customer)
- SUB (SX001G:subContractor)
- AGNT (SX001G:contractAgent)
- ESCR (SX001G:escrowHolder)

Examples
- Contractor
- Subcontractor
- Supplier
- Escrow holder
- Customer

Type
- CDM ClassificationType

82   ContractRelationship

Definition

ContractRelationship is a <<relationship>> where one Contract relates to another Contract.

Reference
- Contract, refer to Para 73

Type
- UML class

83   contractRelationshipType

Definition

contractRelationshipType is a classification that identifies the meaning of the established relationship.

Valid values
- SUBC (SX001G:subContractOf)
- REPC (SX001G:replacesContract)
- RELC (SX001G:relatedContract)
- EXTC (SX001G:extendsContract)

Examples
- subcontract
- replaces
- extends
- associated

Type
- CDM ClassificationType

84 Country

Definition

Country is a self-governing political entity, occupying a particular territory.

Type
- UML class

85 countryCode

Definition

countryCode is a string of characters used to uniquely identify a Country and to differentiate it from other instances of Country.

Note

It is advised to use ISO 3166-1 alpha-2.

Reference
- Country, refer to Para 84

Type
- CDM ClassificationType

86 countryName

Definition

countryName is a name by which the Country is known and can be easily referenced.

Reference
- Country, refer to Para 84

Type
- CDM NameType

87 crud

Definition

Acronym for "Create; Read, Update, Delete".

Type
- CDM validValue

88   Cuboid

Definition

`Cuboid` represents a three-dimensional object where all its faces are rectangles and all angles are right angles.

Type

–   UML class

89   Cylinder

Definition

`Cylinder` represents a three-dimensional object with straight parallel sides and a circular section.

Type

–   UML class

Applicable to: All

Page intentionally blank.

Chapter 2.4

Glossary - D

Table of contents

List of tables

References

Table 1 References

Chap No./Document No.	Title
Chap 2.1	Glossary - A
Chap 2.6	Glossary - F
Chap 2.9	Glossary - I
Chap 2.15	Glossary - O
Chap 2.16	Glossary - P
Chap 2.19	Glossary - S
Chap 2.20	Glossary - T
Chap 2.22	Glossary - V

1 Damage Definition UoF

Definition

The Damage Definition UoF provides the capability to define damages that can be induced on a `Product` during its in-service phase.

Reference

- `Product`, refer to Chap 2.16

2 DamageAnalysis

Definition

`DamageAnalysis` is an `AnalysisActivity` that represents the objective for, and outcome of, a damage analysis carried out for the `AnalysisCandidateItem`.

References

- `AnalysisActivity`, refer to Chap 2.1
- `AnalysisCandidateItem`, refer to Chap 2.1

Type

- UML class

3 DamageAnalysisRevision

Definition

`DamageAnalysisRevision` is an `AnalysisActivityRevision` representing an iteration applied to a `DamageAnalysis`.

References

- `AnalysisActivityRevision`, refer to Chap 2.1
- `DamageAnalysis`, refer to Para 2

Type
-   UML class

4   DamageCause

Definition
DamageCause is a <<relationship>> where a DamageDefinition relates to a SpecialEventDefinition that in some way is associated with the damage.

References
-   DamageDefinition, refer to Para 5
-   SpecialEventDefinition, refer to Chap 2.19

Type
-   UML class

5   DamageDefinition

Definition
DamageDefinition is a <<class>> that represents a loss or reduction of functionality due to external causes or use outside specified limits.

Type
-   UML class

6   damageDefinitionDescription

Definition
damageDefinitionDescription is a description that gives more information on the DamageDefinition.

Reference
-   DamageDefinition, refer to Para 5

Type
-   CDM DescriptorType

7   damageDefinitionFamily

Definition
damageDefinitionFamily is a classification that identifies a group of damages which share the damage characteristics and often lead to the same, or similar, corrective action.

Valid values
-   SCR (SX001G:scratchDamageDefinition)
-   DNT (SX001G:dentDamageDefinition)
-   CRK (SX001G:crackDamageDefinition)

Examples
-   Dent
-   Crack
-   Scratch

Type
-   CDM ClassificationType

8   damageDefinitionName

Definition

damageDefinitionName is a name by which the DamageDefinition is known and can be easily referenced.

Reference

- DamageDefinition, refer to Para 5

Type

- CDM NameType

9   DamageImpact

Definition

DamageImpact is a <<relationship>> that defines a consequence resulting from the defined DamageDefinition.

Reference

- DamageDefinition, refer to Para 5

Type

- UML class

10   damageImpactRatio

Definition

damageImpactRatio identifies the fraction of individual occurrences of DamageDefinition that will result in the associated FailureMode in relation to the entire population of occurrences of the DamageDefinition.

References

- DamageDefinition, refer to Para 5
- FailureMode, refer to Chap 2.6

Type

- CDM PropertyType

11   dataModuleIssueInWorkNumber

Definition

dataModuleIssueInWorkNumber is a string of characters used for monitoring and control of intermediate drafts of S1000DDataModuleIssue.

Note

A dataModuleIssueInWorkNumber must be created in accordance with the rules defined in S1000D.

Reference

- S1000DDataModuleIssue, refer to Chap 2.19

Type

- UML string

12   dataModuleIssueLanguage

Definition

`dataModuleIssueLanguage` is a classification that identifies the language used to produce the content of the `S1000DDataModuleIssue`.

Note

A `dataModuleIssueLanguage` must be created in accordance with the rules defined in S1000D.

Reference

- `S1000DDataModuleIssue`, refer to <u>Chap 2.19</u>

Type

- CDM `ClassificationType`

13   dataModuleIssueLanguageCountry

Definition

`dataModuleIssueLanguageCountry` is a classification that identifies the country where the language, identified by `dataModuleIssueLanguage`, is spoken

Note

A `dataModuleIssueLanguageCountry` must be created in accordance with the rules defined in S1000D.

Reference

- `dataModuleIssueLanguage`, refer to <u>Para 12</u>

Type

- CDM `ClassificationType`

14   dataModuleIssueNumber

Definition

`dataModuleIssueNumber` is a string of characters used to identify the release number of the `S1000DDataModuleIssue`

Note

A `dataModuleIssueNumber` must be created in accordance with the rules defined in S1000D.

Reference

- `S1000DDataModuleIssue`, refer to <u>Chap 2.19</u>

Type

- UML string

15   DatedClassification

Definition

`DatedClassification` is a <<compoundAttribute>> that represents a classification in conjunction with its recording date.

Type

- UML class

16   DateRange

Definition

`DateRange` is a <<compoundAttribute>> that identifies an interval of dates.

Note

The range pattern may be open-ended.

Type

– UML class

17   dateRangeEnd

Definition

`dateRangeEnd` is a date that represents the conclusion of the range.

Type

– CDM `DateType`

18   dateRangeStart

Definition

`dateRangeStart` is a date that represents the beginning of the range.

Type

– CDM `DateType`

19   DateTimeRange

Definition

`DateTimeRange` is a <<compoundAttribute>> that identifies an interval of date and times.

Type

– UML class

20   dateTimeRangeEnd

Definition

`dateTimeRangeEnd` is a calendar date and time that represents the culmination of the range.

Type

– CDM `DateTimeType`

21   dateTimeRangeStart

Definition

`dateTimeRangeStart` is a calendar date and time that represents the beginning of the range.

Type

– CDM `DateTimeType`

22   DateTimeType

Definition

`DateTimeType` is an S-Series ILS specifications defined <<primitive>> that extends the `DateType` with the capability to also represent time on a particular day.

Reference

DateType, refer to Para 23

Type

— UML class

23 DateType

Definition

DateType is an S-Series ILS specifications defined <<primitive>> that represent calendar dates.

Type

— UML class

24 dayComponent

Definition

dayComponent is an Integer that represents the day of the month within a year expressed as a value between '1' and '31'.

Reference

— value, refer to Chap 2.22

Type

— UML integer

25 Decision Tree Template Definition UoF

Definition

The Decision Tree Template Definition UoF provides the capability to represent the definition of decision processes which must be followed when performing an actual analysis.

26 DecisionTreeAnalysisItem

Definition

DecisionTreeAnalysisItem is an <<extend>> interface that provides its associated data model to those classes that implement it.

Type

— UML <<extend>> stereotype

27 DecisionTreeTemplate

Definition

DecisionTreeTemplate is a <<class>> that enables the representation of a decision process including a set of defined steps and binary decisions.

Type

— UML class

28 DecisionTreeTemplateActionDefinition

Definition

DecisionTreeTemplateActionDefinition is a <<class>> that specifies actions and/or measures that must be taken as part of the decision process.

Type
- UML class

29   decisionTreeTemplateActionDefinitionDescription

Definition
`decisionTreeTemplateActionDefinitionDescription` is a description that provides further information on the action to be taken.

Type
- CDM `DescriptorType`

30   decisionTreeTemplateActionDefinitionIdentifier

Definition
`decisionTreeTemplateActionDefinitionIdentifier` is an identifier that establishes a unique designator for a `DecisionTreeTemplateActionDefinition` and to differentiate it from other instances of `DecisionTreeTemplateActionDefinition`.

References
- DecisionTreeTemplateActionDefinition, refer to Para 28
- identifier, refer to Chap 2.9

Valid values
- ID (SX001G:decisionTreeTemplateActionDefinitionIdentifier)

Type
- CDM `IdentifierType`

31   decisionTreeTemplateActionDefinitionName

Definition
`decisionTreeTemplateActionDefinitionName` is a name that defines the core action and/or measure to be taken.

Type
- CDM `NameType`

32   decisionTreeTemplateAnalysisDomain

Definition
`decisionTreeTemplateAnalysisDomain` is a name that further specifies the domain for which the `DecisionTreeTemplate` is defined.

Reference
- `DecisionTreeTemplate`, refer to Para 27

Examples
- Gear boxes
- Obsolescence
- In Service Training Optimization
- In Service Support Optimization
- Logistics Support Analysis

Type
- CDM `NameType`

33 decisionTreeTemplateDescription

Definition

`decisionTreeTemplateDescription` is a description that provides more information on the purpose and scope of the defined analysis.

Type
- CDM `DescriptorType`

34 DecisionTreeTemplateEndActionDefinition

Definition

`DecisionTreeTemplateEndActionDefinition` is a `DecisionTreeTemplateActionDefinition` that defines an end action for the decision process.

Reference
- `DecisionTreeTemplateActionDefinition`, refer to Para 28

Type
- UML class

35 DecisionTreeTemplateFollowOnItem

Definition

`DecisionTreeTemplateFollowOnItem` is a <<select>> interface that identifies items which can be selected to define the next step decision process.

Type
- UML <<select>> stereotype

36 DecisionTreeTemplateFurtherAnalysisActionDefinition

Definition

`DecisionTreeTemplateFurtherAnalysisActionDefinition` is a `DecisionTreeTemplateActionDefinition` that will be followed by another question or action.

Reference
- `DecisionTreeTemplateActionDefinition`, refer to Para 28

Type
- UML class

37 decisionTreeTemplateIdentifier

Definition

`decisionTreeTemplateIdentifier` is an identifier that establishes a unique designator for a `DecisionTreeTemplate` and to differentiate it from other instances of `DecisionTreeTemplate`.

References
- `DecisionTreeTemplate`, refer to Para 27
- `identifier`, refer to Chap 2.9

Valid values
- ID (SX001G:decisionTreeTemplateIdentifier)

Type
- CDM `IdentifierType`

38 decisionTreeTemplateName

Definition
decisionTreeTemplateName is a name by which the `DecisionTreeTemplate` is known and can be easily referenced.

Reference
- `DecisionTreeTemplate`, refer to Para 27

Type
- CDM `NameType`

39 DecisionTreeTemplateQuestionDefinition

Definition
`DecisionTreeTemplateQuestionDefinition` is a <<class>> that specifies a question that result in a YES or NO answer.

Type
- UML class

40 decisionTreeTemplateQuestionDefinitionDescription

Definition
`decisionTreeTemplateQuestionDefinitionDescription` is a description that provides further information and clarification on the question to be answered.

Type
- CDM `DescriptorType`

41 decisionTreeTemplateQuestionDefinitionIdentifier

Definition
`decisionTreeTemplateQuestionDefinitionIdentifier` is an identifier that establishes a unique designator for a `DecisionTreeTemplateQuestionDefinition` and to differentiate it from other instances of `DecisionTreeTemplateQuestionDefinition`.

References
- `DecisionTreeTemplateQuestionDefinition`, refer to Para 39
- `identifier`, refer to Chap 2.9

Valid values
- ID (SX001G:decisionTreeTemplateQuestionDefinitionIdentifier)

Type
- CDM `IdentifierType`

42 decisionTreeTemplateQuestionDefinitionName

Definition
`decisionTreeTemplateQuestionDefinitionName` is a name that defines the core question to be answered.

Type
- CDM NameType

43 DecisionTreeTemplateRevision

Definition
DecisionTreeTemplateRevision is a <<class>> representing an iteration applied to a DecisionTreeTemplate.

Reference
- DecisionTreeTemplate, refer to Para 27

Type
- UML class

44 decisionTreeTemplateRevisionDate

Definition
decisionTreeTemplateRevisionDate is a date that specifies when a DecisionTreeTemplateRevision was defined.

Reference
- DecisionTreeTemplateRevision, refer to Para 43

Type
- CDM DateType

45 decisionTreeTemplateRevisionIdentifier

Definition
decisionTreeTemplateRevisionIdentifier is an identifier that establishes a unique designator for a DecisionTreeTemplateRevision and to differentiate it from other instances of DecisionTreeTemplateRevision.

References
- DecisionTreeTemplateRevision, refer to Para 43
- identifier, refer to Chap 2.9

Valid values
- ID (SX001G:decisionTreeTemplateRevisionIdentifier)

Type
- CDM IdentifierType

46 decisionTreeTemplateRevisionRationale

Definition
decisionTreeTemplateRevisionRationale is a description that gives more information on the justification for revising the defined DecisionTreeTemplate.

Reference
- DecisionTreeTemplate, refer to Para 27

Type
- CDM DescriptorType

47 decisionTreeTemplateRevisionStatus

Definition

`decisionTreeTemplateRevisionStatus` is a state that identifies the maturity of a `DecisionTreeTemplateRevision`.

References

- `DecisionTreeTemplateRevision`, refer to Para 43
- `state`, refer to Chap 2.19

Type

- CDM `StateType`

48 DecisionTreeTemplateStartItem

Definition

`DecisionTreeTemplateStartItem` is a <<select>> interface that identifies items which can be selected as the starting point for the decision process.

Type

- UML <<select>> stereotype

49 descriptorLanguage

Definition

`descriptorLanguage` is a word or a code that determines the language in which the `descriptorText` is written.

Reference

- `descriptorText`, refer to Para 52

Type

- CDM `validValue`

50 descriptorProvidedBy

Definition

`descriptorProvidedBy` identifies the Organization that provided the `descriptorText`.

References

- `Organization`, refer to Chap 2.15
- `descriptorText`, refer to Para 52

Type

- CDM `Organization`

51 descriptorProvidedDate

Definition

`descriptorProvidedDate` is a date that defines when the `descriptorText` was provided.

Reference

- `descriptorText`, refer to Para 52

Type
- CDM `DateType`

52 descriptorText

Definition

`descriptorText` is a string of characters that provides the textual data.

Type
- UML string

53 DescriptorType

Definition

`DescriptorType` is an S-Series ILS specifications defined <<primitive>> that represents any form of textual data (free form) along with its core characterizations.

Type
- UML class

54 Design Change Request UoF

Definition

The Design Change Request UoF provides the capability to identify proposed changes against items including the rationale for this change.

55 diameter

Definition

`diameter` is a property that specifies the longitudinal dimension of a circular section when measured through its center.

Type
- CDM `PropertyType`

56 Digital File UoF

Definition

The Digital File UoF provides the capability to both reference a digital file from the exchanged data as well as to exchange the digital file itself.

57 DigitalFile

Definition

`DigitalFile` is a <<class>> that provides the identification of data stored on an electronic device that can be interpreted by a computer.

Type
- UML class

58 digitalFileContentClass

Definition

`digitalFileContentClass` is a classification that determine the meaning of the information within the `DigitalFile`.

Reference
- `DigitalFile`, refer to Para 57

Valid values
- MOV (SX001G:movieFileContent)
- DRW (SX001G:drawingFileContent)
- SOU (SX001G:soundFileContent)
- VID (SX001G:videoFileContent)
- HUM (SX001G:healthAndUsageDataFileContent)
- INS (SX001G:instructionsFileContent)
- MAN (SX001G:manualFileContent)
- BIT (SX001G:builtInTestFileContent)
- TST (SX001G:testResultsFileContent)
- OTH (SX001G:otherFileContent)
- INV (SX001G:invoiceFileContent)
- PRB (SX001G:problemReportFileContent)
- CSW (SX001G:coursewareFileContent)
- AUD (SX001G:audioFileContent)
- PHO (SX001G:photographFileContent)
- REP (SX001G:reportFileContent)
- SCH (SX001G:schematicsFileContent)
- WIR (SX001G:wiringFileContent)
- PUB (SX001G:publicationFileContent)
- 3D (SX001G:3dModelFileContent)

Type
- CDM `ClassificationType`

59 digitalFileContentDescription

Definition

`digitalFileContentDescription` is a phrase that gives more details about the information contained in the `DigitalFile`

Reference
- `DigitalFile`, refer to Para 57

Type
- CDM `DescriptorType`

60 digitalFileLocator

Definition

`digitalFileLocator` is an identifier that establishes a unique designator for a `DigitalFile` used to locate and identify a `DigitalFile` and to differentiate it from other instances of `DigitalFile`.

References
- `DigitalFile`, refer to Para 57
- `identifier`, refer to Chap 2.9

Valid values
- ID (SX001G:digitalFileLocator)

Type
- CDM `IdentifierType`

61   DigitalFileReference

Definition

`DigitalFileReference` is a <<relationship>> that allows a `DigitalFile` to reference a `DigitalFileReferencedItem`.

References
- `DigitalFile`, refer to Para 57
- `DigitalFileReferencedItem`, refer to Para 62

Type
- UML class

62   DigitalFileReferencedItem

Definition

`DigitalFileReferencedItem` is a <<select>> interface that identifies an item which in some way is associated with the content of the `DigitalFile`.

Reference
- `DigitalFile`, refer to Para 57

Type
- UML <<select>> stereotype

63   digitalFileReferenceJustification

Definition

`digitalFileReferenceJustification` is a description that provides more on information on the reason why the `DigitalFileReferencedItem` is referenced.

Reference
- `DigitalFileReferencedItem`, refer to Para 62

Example
- Crack discovered on `BreakdownElement` ABC-123

Type
- CDM `DescriptorType`

64   DigitalFileReferencingItem

Definition

`DigitalFileReferencingItem` is an <<extend>> interface that provides its associated data model to those classes that implement it.

Type
- UML <<extend>> stereotype

65   digitalFileRepresentation

Definition

`digitalFileRepresentation` is a string of characters representing the content of the `DigitalFile`.

Reference
- `DigitalFile`, refer to Para 57

Example
- A uuencoded ASCII `umlString` representing a binary source file.

Type
- UML string

66   digitalFileType

Definition
`digitalFileType` is a classification that specifies the format of the data within the `DigitalFile`.

Note
Typically, the file name extension in Microsoft Windows.

Reference
- `DigitalFile`, refer to <u>Para 57</u>

Valid values
- DOCX (SX001G:microsoftWordFormatFileType)
- DAT (SX001G:dataFormatFileType)
- XSD (SX001G:xmlSchemaDefinitionFileType)
- XLS (SX001G:microsoftExcelFormatFileType)
- XLSX (SX001G:microsoftExcelFormatFileType)
- HTM (SX001G:hyperTextMarkupLanguageFileType)
- ODS (SX001G:openDocumentSpreadsheetFileType)
- ODT (SX001G:openDocumentTextFileType)
- DOC (SX001G:microsoftWordFormatFileType)
- PDF (SX001G:portableDocumentFormatFileType)
- TIFF (SX001G:taggedImageFileFormatFileType)
- UNK (SX001G:unknownFileType)
- ASF (SX001G:advanceSystemsFormatFileType)
- PNG (SX001G:portableNetworkGraphicsFileType)
- MPEG (SX001G:motionPictureExpertsGroupMovieFileType)
- TXT (SX001G:textFileType)
- WAV (SX001G:waveformAudioFileType)
- MP3 (SX001G:mp3AudioFileType)
- RAW (SX001G:rawSampleAudioFileType)
- MOV (SX001G:quickTimeMovieFileType)
- EDF (SX001G:europeanDataFormatSigalFileType)
- CGM (SX001G:computerGraphicsMetafileFileType)
- BIN (SX001G:binaryFileType)
- JPEG (SX001G:jointPhotographicExpertsGroupFileType)
- AVI (SX001G:audioVideoInterleavedFileType)
- OTH (SX001G:otherFileType)

Type
- CDM `ClassificationType`

67   disassemblyCode

Definition
`disassemblyCode` is a string of characters that represents the disassembly code attribute of the data module code.

Note

A `disassemblyCode` must be created in accordance with the rules defined in S1000D.

Type
– UML string

68 disassemblyCodeVariant

Definition

`disassemblyCodeVariant` is a string of characters that represents the disassembly code variant attribute of the data module code.

Note

A `disassemblyCodeVariant` must be created in accordance with the rules defined in S1000D.

Type
– UML string

69 DiscreteTimeLimit

Definition

`DiscreteTimeLimit` is a `TimeLimit` that is distinct, where its next possible occurrence cannot be scheduled.

Note 1

A "trigger" is something that activates a `DiscreteTimeLimit`.

Note 2

A "threshold" is a point that must not be exceeded once the `DiscreteTimeLimit` has been activated. If there is no threshold value, then the `TimeLimitItem` must be initiated immediately after the `DiscreteTimeLimit` activation.

Reference
– `TimeLimit`, refer to Chap 2.20

Type
– UML class

70 DMEWG

Definition

Data Modeling and Exchange Working Group

Type
– Acronym

71 Document

Definition

`Document` is a <<class>> that represents a compiled set of information that serves a purpose.

Examples
– drawing
– report
– manual

Type
- UML class

72   Document UoF

Definition
The Document UoF provides the capability to identify a physical document or a digital file and their associated metadata.

Reference
- Document, refer to Para 70

73   documentIdentifier

Definition
documentIdentifier is an identifier that establishes a unique designator for a Document and to differentiate it from other instances of Document.

References
- Document, refer to Para 70
- identifier, refer to Chap 2.9

Valid values
- ID (SX001G:documentIdentifier)

Type
- CDM IdentifierType

74   DocumentIssue

Definition
DocumentIssue is a <<class>> that represents a specific release of a Document

Reference
- Document, refer to Para 70

Type
- UML class

75   documentIssueDate

Definition
documentIssueDate is a date that defines when a specific issue of a document was released.

Type
- CDM DateType

76   documentIssueIdentifier

Definition
documentIssueIdentifier is an identifier that establishes a unique designator for a DocumentIssue and to differentiate it from other instances of DocumentIssue.

References
- DocumentIssue, refer to Para 74
- identifier, refer to Chap 2.9

Valid values
- ID (SX001G:documentIssueIdentifier)

Type
- CDM IdentifierType

77 documentIssueRationale

Definition
documentIssueRationale is a description that gives more information on the justification for revising the Document.

Reference
- Document, refer to Para 70

Type
- CDM DescriptorType

78 documentIssueStatus

Definition
documentIssueStatus is a state that identifies the maturity of a DocumentIssue.

References
- DocumentIssue, refer to Para 74
- state, refer to Chap 2.19

Valid values
- IN (SX001G:InititedDocumentIssueStatus)
- IP (SX001G:InProgressDocumentIssueStatus)
- A (SX001G:ApprovedDocumentIssueStatus)
- R (SX001G:ReleasedDocumentIssueStatus)
- C (SX001G:CancelledDocumentIssueStatus)
- S (SX001G:SuspendedDocumentIssueStatus)

Type
- CDM StateType

79 DocumentItem

Definition
DocumentItem is a <<select>> interface that identifies items which can be selected as Document.

Reference
- Document, refer to Para 70

Type
- UML <<select>> stereotype

80 DocumentReferencingItem

Definition
DocumentReferencingItem is an <<extend>> interface that provides its associated data model to those classes that implement it.

Type

– UML <<extend>> stereotype

81   documentTitle

Definition

documentTitle is a name by which the Document is known and can be easily referenced.

Reference

– Document, refer to Para 70

Type

– CDM NameType

82   documentType

Definition

documentType is a classification that identifies the category of the Document.

Reference

– Document, refer to Para 70

Valid values

– STD (SX001G:standardsDocument)
– SPEC (SX001G:specificationDocument)
– TR (SX001G:technicalReport)
– DRW (SX001G:drawingDocument)
– TMAN (SX001G:technicalManual)
– PCAT (SX001G:partsCatalogueDocument)

Type

– CDM ClassificationType

Page intentionally blank.

Chapter 2.5

Glossary - E

Table of contents

Page

List of tables

References

Table 1 References

Chap No./Document No.	Title
Chap 2.1	Glossary - A
Chap 2.2	Glossary - B
Chap 2.9	Glossary - I
Chap 2.15	Glossary - O
Chap 2.16	Glossary - P
Chap 2.19	Glossary - S
Chap 2.20	Glossary - T
Chap 2.22	Glossary - V

1 EffectiveOnProductConfiguration

Definition

`EffectiveOnProductConfiguration` is a <<relationship>> that identifies that a `EffectiveOnProductConfigurationItem`, included in the Breakdown for the overall `Product`, is effective in the associated `AllowedProductConfiguration`.

References

- `AllowedProductConfiguration`, refer to Chap 2.1
- `Breakdown`, refer to Chap 2.2
- `EffectiveOnProductConfigurationItem`, refer to Para 2
- `Product`, refer to Chap 2.16

Type

- UML class

2 EffectiveOnProductConfigurationItem

Definition

`EffectiveOnProductConfigurationItem` is an <<extend>> interface that provides its associated data model to those classes that can be included in one or many instances of `AllowedProductConfiguration`.

Reference

- `AllowedProductConfiguration`, refer to Chap 2.1

Type

- UML <<extend>> stereotype

3 End user

Definition

Refer to user and operator

Note
Use either the term user or the term operator depending on what is meant by end user in the specific context.

Reference
- Operator, refer to Chap 2.15
- User, refer to Chap 2.21

Type
- Business Term

4   Environment Definition UoF

Definition
The Environment Definition UoF provides the capability to define circumstances, objects, events and/or conditions by which something can be surrounded and that influence the performance of an associated item.

5   EnvironmentDefinition

Definition
`EnvironmentDefinition` is a <<class>> that specifies the circumstances, objects, events and/or conditions by which something can be surrounded and that influence the performance of an associated item.

Type
- UML class

6   EnvironmentDefinitionCharacteristic

Definition
`EnvironmentDefinitionCharacteristic` is a <<class>> that represents a measurable or observable characteristic for a circumstance, object, event or condition that is significant to the `EnvironmentDefinition`.

Reference
- `EnvironmentDefinition`, refer to Para 5

Type
- UML class

7   environmentDefinitionCharacteristicDescription

Definition
`environmentDefinitionCharacteristicDescription` is a description that gives more information on the `EnvironmentDefinitionCharacteristic`.

Reference
- `EnvironmentDefinitionCharacteristic`, refer to Para 5

Type
- CDM `DescriptorType`

8   environmentDefinitionCharacteristicName

Definition

`environmentDefinitionCharacteristicName` is a name by which the `EnvironmentDefinitionCharacteristic` is known and can be easily referenced.

Reference

- `EnvironmentDefinitionCharacteristic`, refer to Para 6

Type

- CDM `NameType`

9   environmentDefinitionCharacteristicValue

Definition

`environmentDefinitionCharacteristicValue` is a property that represents a measurable or observable characteristic for a circumstance, object, event or condition that is typical to the `EnvironmentDefinition`.

Reference

- `EnvironmentDefinition`, refer to Para 5

Type

- CDM `PropertyType`

10   environmentDefinitionCharacteristicValueComparisonOperator

Definition

`environmentDefinitionCharacteristicValueComparisonOperator` is a classification that identifies the comparison operator which is to be used in order to qualify whether an actual environment is as a member of the defined `EnvironmentDefinition`.

Reference

- `EnvironmentDefinition`, refer to Para 5

Type

- CDM `ClassificationType`

11   environmentDefinitionDescription

Definition

`environmentDefinitionDescription` is a description that gives more information on the `EnvironmentDefinition`.

Reference

- `EnvironmentDefinition`, refer to Para 5

Type

- CDM `DescriptorType`

12   environmentDefinitionIdentifier

Definition

`environmentDefinitionIdentifier` is an `identifier` that establishes a unique designator for an `EnvironmentDefinition` and to differentiate it from other instances of `EnvironmentDefinition`.

References

- `EnvironmentDefinition`, refer to Para 5
- `identifier`, refer to Chap 2.9

Valid values

- ID (SX001G:environmentDefinitionIdentifier)

Type

- CDM `IdentifierType`

13   EnvironmentDefinitionItem

Definition

`EnvironmentDefinitionItem` is an <<extend>> interface that provides its associated data model to those classes that implement it.

Type

- UML <<extend>> stereotype

14   environmentDefinitionName

Definition

`environmentDefinitionName` is a name by which the `EnvironmentDefinition` is known and can be easily referenced.

Reference

- `EnvironmentDefinition`, refer to Para 5

Type

- CDM `NameType`

15   EnvironmentDefinitionRelationship

Definition

`EnvironmentDefinitionRelationship` is a <<relationship>> where one `EnvironmentDefinition` relates to another `EnvironmentDefinition`.

Reference

- `EnvironmentDefinition`, refer to Para 5

Type

- UML class

16   environmentDefinitionRelationshipType

Definition

`environmentDefinitionRelationshipType` is a classification that identifies the meaning of the established relationship.

Valid values
- SSNL (SX001G:seasonalEnvironmentDefinitionVariation)
- SPEC (SX001G:specializationOfEnvironmentDefinition)

Type
- CDM `ClassificationType`

17 EnvironmentDefinitionRevision

Definition

`EnvironmentDefinitionRevision` is a <<class>> representing an iteration applied to an `EnvironmentDefinition`.

Reference
- `EnvironmentDefinition`, refer to Para 5

Type
- UML class

18 environmentDefinitionRevisionDate

Definition

`environmentDefinitionRevisionDate` is a date that specifies when the `EnvironmentDefinition` was revised.

Reference
- `EnvironmentDefinition`, refer to Para 5

Type
- CDM `DateType`

19 environmentDefinitionRevisionIdentifier

Definition

`environmentDefinitionRevisionIdentifier` is an `identifier` that establishes a unique designator for a `EnvironmentDefinitionRevision` and to differentiate it from other instances of `EnvironmentDefinitionRevision`.

References
- `EnvironmentDefinitionRevision`, refer to Para 17
- `identifier`, refer to Chap 2.9

Valid values
- ID (SX001G:environmentDefinitionRevisionIdentifier)

Type
- CDM `IdentifierType`

20 environmentDefinitionRevisionRationale

Definition

`environmentDefinitionRevisionRationale` is a description that provides a justification for revising the `EnvironmentDefinition`.

Reference
- `EnvironmentDefinition`, refer to Para 5

Type
- CDM `DescriptorType`

21   environmentDefinitionRevisionStatus

Definition
`environmentDefinitionRevisionStatus` is a state that identifies the maturity of
an `EnvironmentDefinitionRevision`.

References
- `EnvironmentDefinitionRevision`, refer to Para 17
- state, refer to Chap 2.19

Type
- CDM `StateType`

22   EvaluationByAssertionOfClassInstance

Definition
`EvaluationByAssertionOfClassInstance` is an `EvaluationCriteria`
that identifies a class instance to be used as an assert item and be mapped to a Boolean
expression which can be evaluated to be either TRUE or FALSE.

Reference
- `EvaluationCriteria`, refer to Para 27

Type
- UML class

23   EvaluationByAssertionOfCondition

Definition
`EvaluationByAssertionOfCondition` is an `EvaluationCriteria` that
identifies a combination of a defined condition and a defined value to be used as an assert item
and be mapped to a Boolean expression which can be evaluated to be either TRUE or FALSE.

References
- `EvaluationCriteria`, refer to Para 27
- value, refer to Chap 2.22

Type
- UML class

24   EvaluationByAssertionOfSerializedItems

Definition
`EvaluationByAssertionOfSerializedItems` is an
`EvaluationCriteria` that identifies a class instance together with an associated serial
number range to be used as an assert item and be mapped to a Boolean expression which can
be evaluated to be either TRUE or FALSE.

Reference
- `EvaluationCriteria`, refer to Para 27

Type
- UML class

25 evaluationByAssertionRole

Definition

`evaluationByAssertionRole` is a classification that defines the context in which the `EvaluationByAssertionOfClassInstance` is being referenced.

Reference

`EvaluationByAssertionOfClassInstance`, refer to Para 22

Valid values

- CUS (SX001G:customer)
- OP (SX001G:operator)

Type

- CDM `ClassificationType`

26 EvaluationByNestedApplicabilityStatement

Definition

`EvaluationByNestedApplicabilityStatement` is an `EvaluationCriteria` that enables an `ApplicabilityStatement` to be reused as part of this `EvaluationCriteria`.

Note

This class enables the definition of nested applicability statements.

References

- `ApplicabilityStatement`, refer to Chap 2.1
- `EvaluationCriteria`, refer to Para 27

Type

- UML class

27 EvaluationCriteria

Definition

`EvaluationCriteria` is a <<class>> that defines conditions that can be mapped to a Boolean expression which can be evaluated to be either TRUE or FALSE.

Type

- UML class

28 EventThresholdDefinition

Definition

`EventThresholdDefinition` is a `ThresholdDefinition` that is driven by occurrences of related `TimeLimitEventItems`.

Reference

`ThresholdDefinition`, refer to Chap 2.20

Type

- UML class

29   eventThresholdNumberOfEventOccurrences

Definition

eventThresholdNumberOfEventOccurrences is an integer that defines how many times an event must be repeated for the EventThresholdDefinition to be activated.

Reference

- EventThresholdDefinition, refer to Para 28

Type

- UML integer

30   extensionCode

Definition

extensionCode is a string of characters used to identify the organization receiving the customized data module.

Note 1

An extensionCode must be created in accordance with the rules defined in S1000D.

Note 2

An extensionCode must be created in accordance with the rules defined in S1000D.

Type

- UML string

31   extensionProducer

Definition

extensionProducer is a string of characters used to identify the organization providing the customized data module.

Note 1

An extensionProducer must be created in accordance with the rules defined in S1000D.

Note 2

An extensionProducer must be created in accordance with the rules defined in S1000D.

Type

- UML string

Page intentionally blank.

Chapter 2.6

Glossary - F

Table of contents

List of tables

References

Table 1 References

Chap No./Document No.	Title
Chap 2.4	Glossary - D
Chap 2.9	Glossary - I
Chap 2.12	Glossary - L
Chap 2.19	Glossary - S

1   Facility

Definition

Facility is a <<class>> that represents a physically limited infrastructure which exists, or is intended to be built or installed, and is established to serve a particular purpose.

Type
–   UML class

2   Facility UoF

Definition

The Facility UoF provides the capability to identify a facility and to declare to what extent it fulfills a set of identified infrastructure requirements.

Reference
–   Facility, refer to Para 1

3   facilityDescription

Definition

facilityDescription is a description that gives more information on capabilities provided by the Facility.

Reference
- Facility, refer to Para 1

Type
- CDM DescriptorType

4   facilityIdentifier

Definition
facilityIdentifier is an identifier that establishes a unique designator for a Facility and to differentiate it from other instances of Facility.

References
- Facility, refer to Para 1
- identifier, refer to Chap 2.9

Valid values
- ID (SX001G:facilityIdentifier)
- L (SX001G:legalFacilityIdentifier)
- O (SX001G:ownerAssignedFacilityIdentifier)

Type
- CDM IdentifierType

5   FacilityLocation

Definition
FacilityLocation is a <<relationship>> that defines the past, present or future Location for the Facility.

References
- Facility, refer to Para 1
- Location, refer to Chap 2.12

Type
- UML class

6   facilityLocationIdentifier

Definition
facilityLocationIdentifier is an identifier that establishes a unique designator for a FacilityLocation and to differentiate it from other instances of FacilityLocation.

References
- FacilityLocation, refer to Para 5
- identifier, refer to Chap 2.9

Valid values
- ID (SX001G:facilityLocationIdentifier)
- SEQ (SX001G:facilityLocationSequenceIdentifier)

Type
- CDM IdentifierType

7 facilityLocationPeriod

Definition

`facilityLocationPeriod` is a date range that defines the date interval during which a `Facility` is located at a specific `Location`.

References
- `Facility`, refer to Para 1
- `Location`, refer to Chap 2.12

Type
- CDM `DateRange`

8 facilityName

Definition

`facilityName` is a name by which the `Facility` is known and can be easily referenced.

Reference
- `Facility`, refer to Para 1

Type
- CDM `NameType`

9 FacilityOperator

Definition

`FacilityOperator` is a <<relationship>> that identifies the party responsible for running the `Facility`.

Reference
- `Facility`, refer to Para 1

Example
- The `FacilityOperator` has leased the `Facility` from the `FacilityOwner`.

Type
- UML class

10 FacilityOperatorItem

Definition

`FacilityOperatorItem` is a <<select>> interface that identifies classes from which an instance can be selected to be the `FacilityOperator`.

Reference
- `FacilityOperator`, refer to Para 9

Type
- UML <<select>> stereotype

11 FacilityRelationship

Definition

`FacilityRelationship` is a <<relationship>> where one `Facility` relates to another `Facility`.

Reference
- `Facility`, refer to <u>Para 1</u>

Type
- UML class

12 facilityRelationshipType

Definition
`facilityRelationshipType` is a classification that identifies the meaning of the
established relationship.

Valid values
- INCL (SX001G:includesFacility)

Type
- CDM `ClassificationType`

13 Failure Mode UoF

Definition
The Failure Mode UoF provides the capability to define the failure modes, their causes and
effects.

14 FailureMode

Definition
`FailureMode` is a <<class>> that defines a functional consequence of an unacceptable
state of the `FailureModeAnalysisItem`.

References
- `FailureModeAnalysisItem`, refer to <u>Para 17</u>
- `state`, refer to <u>Chap 2.19</u>

Example
- No output from electrical circuit.

Type
- UML class

15 FailureModeAnalysis

Definition
`FailureModeAnalysis` is a <<class>> that represents failure modes, effects and
criticality identified for the associated `FailureModeAnalysisItem`.

Reference
- `FailureModeAnalysisItem`, refer to <u>Para 17</u>

Type
- UML class

16 failureModeAnalysisDescription

Definition
`failureModeAnalysisDescription` is a description that gives more information on
the `FailureModeAnalysis`.

Reference
FailureModeAnalysis, refer to Para 15

Example
- The failureModeAnalysisDescription can give further information on background and scope.

Type
- CDM DescriptorType

17 FailureModeAnalysisItem

Definition
FailureModeAnalysisItem is an <<extend>> interface that provides its associated data model to those classes that can have an associated FailureModeAnalysis.

Reference
- FailureModeAnalysis, refer to Para 15

Type
- UML <<extend>> stereotype

18 FailureModeAnalysisRevision

Definition
FailureModeAnalysisRevision is a <<class>> representing an iteration applied to a FailureModeAnalysis.

Reference
- FailureModeAnalysis, refer to Para 15

Type
- UML class

19 failureModeAnalysisRevisionDate

Definition
failureModeAnalysisRevisionDate is a date that specifies when the FailureModeAnalysis was revised.

Reference
- FailureModeAnalysis, refer to Para 15

Type
- CDM DateType

20 failureModeAnalysisRevisionIdentifier

Definition
failureModeAnalysisRevisionIdentifier is an identifier that establishes a unique designator for a FailureModeRevision and to differentiate it from other instances of FailureModeRevision.

Reference
- identifier, refer to Chap 2.9

Valid values
- ID (SX001G:failureModeAnalysisRevisionIdentifier)

Type
- CDM `IdentifierType`

21 failureModeAnalysisRevisionRationale

Definition
`failureModeAnalysisRevisionRationale` is a description that gives more information on the justification for revising the `FailureModeAnalysis`.

Reference
- `FailureModeAnalysis`, refer to Para 15

Type
- CDM `DescriptorType`

22 failureModeAnalysisRevisionStatus

Definition
`failureModeAnalysisRevisionStatus` is a state that identifies the maturity of a `FailureModeAnalysisRevision`.

References
- `FailureModeAnalysisRevision`, refer to Para 18
- `state`, refer to Chap 2.19

Type
- CDM `StateType`

23 failureModeAnalysisType

Definition
`failureModeAnalysisType` is a classification that identifies further specialization for `FailureModeAnalysis`.

Reference
- `FailureModeAnalysis`, refer to Para 15

Valid values
- F (SX001G:systemFunctionFailureModeAnalysis)
- E (SX001G:equipmentFailureModeAnalysis)

Type
- CDM `ClassificationType`

24 FailureModeCause

Definition
`FailureModeCause` is a <<class>> that specifies the physical or chemical process(es) that is the reason for the `FailureMode`.

Reference
- `FailureMode`, refer to Para 14

Type
- UML class

25   failureModeCauseDescription

Definition
`failureModeCauseDescription` is a description that gives more information on the `FailureModeCause`.

Reference
- `FailureModeCause`, refer to Para 24

Type
- CDM `DescriptorType`

26   failureModeCauseIdentifier

Definition
`failureModeCauseIdentifier` is an identifier that establishes a unique designator for a `FailureModeCause` and to differentiate it from other instances of `FailureModeCause`.

References
- `FailureModeCause`, refer to Para 24
- `identifier`, refer to Chap 2.9

Valid values
- ID (SX001G:failureModeCauseIdentifier)

Type
- CDM `IdentifierType`

27   FailureModeCauseItem

Definition
`FailureModeCauseItem` is a <<select>> interface that identifies items which can be selected as being associated with a `FailureModeCause`.

Reference
- `FailureModeCause`, refer to Para 24

Type
- UML <<select>> stereotype

28   FailureModeCauseItemRelationship

Definition
`FailureModeCauseItemRelationship` is a <<relationship>> where a `FailureModeCause` relates to the `FailureModeCauseItem` that in some way is associated with the `FailureModeCause`.

References
- `FailureModeCause`, refer to Para 24
- `FailureModeCauseItem`, refer to Para 27

Type
- UML class

29   failureModeCauseItemRelationshipType

Definition
`failureModeCauseItemRelationshipType` is a classification that identifies the meaning of the established relationship.

Valid values
- A (SX001G:failureCauseAffectedItem)
- C (SX001G:failureCauseConsequenceOf)

Type
- CDM `ClassificationType`

30   failureModeCauseRatio

Definition
`failureModeCauseRatio` identifies the fraction of an individual `FailureModeCause` in relation to the entire population of `FailureModeCauses` identified for the `FailureMode`.

References
- `FailureMode`, refer to Para 14
- `FailureModeCause`, refer to Para 24

Type
- CDM `PropertyType`

31   FailureModeCompensatingProvision

Definition
`FailureModeCompensatingProvision` is a <<class> that represents actions taken to negate or reduce the effect of a failure.

Type
- UML class

32   failureModeCompensatingProvisionCategory

Definition
`failureModeCompensatingProvisionCategory` is a classification that identifies a generalization that organize compensating provisions into an overarching compensating provision taxonomy.

Valid values
- A (SX001G:activeRedundantProvision)
- S (SX001G:standbyRedundantProvision)
- M (SX001G:manualOverrideProvision)

Type
- CDM `ClassificationType`

33   failureModeCompensatingProvisionDescription

Definition

`failureModeCompensatingProvisionDescription` is a description that gives more information on the action taken to negate or reduce the effect of the `FailureMode`.

Reference

- `FailureMode`, refer to Para 14

Type

- CDM `DescriptorType`

34   failureModeCompensatingProvisionIdentifier

Definition

`failureModeCompensatingProvisionIdentifier` is an identifier that establishes a unique designator for a `FailureModeCompensatingProvision` and to differentiate it from other instances of `FailureModeCompensatingProvision`.

References

- `FailureModeCompensatingProvision`, refer to Para 31
- `identifier`, refer to Chap 2.9

Type

- CDM `IdentifierType`

35   failureModeCriticality

Definition

`failureModeCriticality` is a classification that identifies the most serious impact that the `FailureMode` will have on the referred item.

Reference

- `FailureMode`, refer to Para 14

Valid values

- I (SX001G:catastrophicFailureModeConsequence)
- II (SX001G:criticalFailureModeConsequence)
- III (SX001G:marginalFailureModeConsequence)
- IV (SX001G:negligibleFailureModeConsequence)

Type

- CDM `ClassificationType`

36   failureModeDescription

Definition

`failureModeDescription` is a description that gives more information on the `FailureMode`.

Reference

- `FailureMode`, refer to Para 14

Type

- CDM `DescriptorType`

37 FailureModeEffect

Definition

FailureModeEffect is a <<class>> that defines the consequences of an identified FailureMode on the operation, function, or status for the referred item.

Reference
- FailureMode, refer to Para 14

Type
- UML class

38 failureModeEffectDescription

Definition

failureModeEffectDescription is a description that gives more information on the FailureModeEffect.

Reference
- FailureModeEffect, refer to Para 37

Type
- CDM DescriptorType

39 FailureModeEffectItem

Definition

FailureModeEffectItem is a <<select>> interface that identifies items which can be selected as being affected by a FailureMode.

Reference
- FailureMode, refer to Para 14

Type
- UML <<select>> stereotype

40 FailureModeEffectItemRelationship

Definition

FailureModeEffectItemRelationship is a <<relationship>> where a FailureModeEffect relates to the FailureModeEffectItem that is affected by the FailureMode.

References
- FailureMode, refer to Para 14
- FailureModeEffect, refer to Para 37
- FailureModeEffectItem, refer to Para 39

Type
- UML class

41 failureModeEffectLevel

Definition

failureModeEffectLevel is classification that identifies the higher indenture level that will be affected by the FailureMode.

Reference
- FailureMode, refer to Para 14

Valid values
- N (SX001G:nextHigherFailureModeEffect)
- L (SX001G:localFailureModeEffect)
- E (SX001G:systemEndItemFailureModeEffect)
- H (SX001G:higherFailureModeEffect)

Type
- CDM ClassificationType

42   failureModeEffectName

Definition
failureModeEffectName is a name by which the FailureModeEffect is known and can be easily referenced.

Reference
- FailureModeEffect, refer to Para 37

Type
- CDM NameType

43   failureModeIdentifier

Definition
failureModeIdentifier is an identifier that establishes a unique designator for a FailureMode and to differentiate it from other instances of FailureMode.

References
- FailureMode, refer to Para 14
- identifier, refer to Chap 2.9

Valid values
- ID (SX001G:failureModeIdentifier)

Type
- CDM IdentifierType

44   failureModeName

Definition
failureModeName is a name by which the FailureMode is known and can be easily referenced.

Reference
- FailureMode, refer to Para 14

Type
- CDM NameType

45   failureModeRatio

Definition

`failureModeRatio` identifies the fraction of an individual `FailureMode` in relation to the entire population of `FailureModes` identified for the `FailureModeAnalysisItem`.

Note

If the `failureModeRatio` equals '0' then the failure mode is only driven by damages.

References

- `FailureMode`, refer to Para 14
- `FailureModeAnalysisItem`, refer to Para 17

Type

- CDM `PropertyType`

46   FinalInServiceOptimizationAnalysisStep

Definition

`FinalInServiceOptimizationAnalysisStep` is an `InServiceOptimizationAnalysisStep` that specifies final actions and measures taken together with the decision process conclusion and recommendations.

Reference

- `InServiceOptimizationAnalysisStep`, refer to Chap 2.9

Type

- UML class

47   FMEA

Definition

Failure Modes and Effects Analysis.

Type

- Acronym

48   FMECA

Definition

Failure Mode, Effects and Criticality Analysis.

Type

- Acronym

49   FollowOnInServiceOptimizationAnalysis

Definition

`FollowOnInServiceOptimizationAnalysis` is a <<relationship>> where the outcome from the `InServiceOptimizationAnalysis` resulted in an additional `InServiceOptimizationAnalysis`.

Reference

- `InServiceOptimizationAnalysis`, refer to Chap 2.9

Type

- UML class

50 followOnInServiceOptimizationAnalysisRationale

Definition

`followOnInServiceOptimizationAnalysisRationale` is a description that gives more information on the reason for the additionally initiated `InServiceOptimizationAnalysis`.

Reference

- `InServiceOptimizationAnalysis`, refer to Chap 2.9

Type

- CDM `DescriptorType`

51 FurtherAnalysisInServiceOptimizationAnalysisStep

Definition

`FurtherAnalysisInServiceOptimizationAnalysisStep` is an `InServiceOptimizationAnalysisStep` that specifies actions and measures taken before continuing to the next step defined in the associated `DecisionTreeTemplate`.

References

- `DecisionTreeTemplate`, refer to Chap 2.4
- `InServiceOptimizationAnalysisStep`, refer to Chap 2.9

Type

- UML class

Chapter 2.7

Glossary - G

Table of contents
Page

List of tables

References

Table 1 References

Chap No./Document No.	Title
Chap 2.12	Glossary - L
Chap 2.19	Glossary - S

1   GEIA

Definition
Government Electronics & Information Technology Association

Type
– Acronym

2   GeographicalArea

Definition
GeographicalArea is a <<class>> that represents a particular extent of space.

Type
– UML class

3   geographicalAreaDescription

Definition
geographicalAreaDescription is a description that provides more information about the GeographicalArea.

Reference
- `GeographicalArea`, refer to <u>Para 1</u>

Type
- CDM `DescriptorType`

4   geographicalAreaName

Definition
`geographicalAreaName` is a name by which the `GeographicalArea` is known and can be easily referenced.

Reference
- `GeographicalArea`, refer to <u>Para 1</u>

Examples
- Central alps
- Gobi desert
- Dade county
- Tokyo
- Europe
- USA

Type
- CDM `NameType`

5   geographicalAreaType

Definition
`geographicalAreaType` is a classification that identifies the nature of the `GeographicalArea`.

Reference
- `GeographicalArea`, refer to <u>Para 1</u>

Valid values
- CON (SX001G:continent)
- REG (SX001G:geographicalRegion)
- ADM (SX001G:administrativeRegion)
- CITY (SX001G:city)
- MUL (SX001G:multiGeographicalArea)
- DES (SX001G:desert)
- SEA (SX001G:sea)
- OCE (SX001G:ocean)
- CTYG (SX001G:countryGroup)
- LND (SX001G:landmark)
- MOU (SX001G:mountainRange)
- LAN (SX001G:landmass)
- ISL (SX001G:island)

Type
- CDM `ClassificationType`

6   geographicalCoordinateSystem

Definition

`geographicalCoordinateSystem` is a classification that identifies the geographical coordinate system used to determine latitude and longitude.

References
- `latitude`, refer to Chap 2.12
- `longitude`, refer to Chap 2.12
- `system`, refer to Chap 2.19

Valid values
- DMS (SX001G:degreeMinutesSecondsGeographicalCoordinateSystem)
- DD (SX001G:decimalDegreeGeographicalCoordinateSystem)

Type
- CDM `ClassificationType`

7   GlobalPosition

Definition

`GlobalPosition` is a <<class>> that identifies a point in space by a set of coordinates.

Type
- UML class

Page intentionally blank.

Chapter 2.8

Glossary - H

Table of contents

Page

List of tables

References

Table 1 References

Chap No./Document No.	Title
Chap 2.2	Glossary - B
Chap 2.16	Glossary - P
Chap 2.22	Glossary - V

1   Hardware Element UoF

Definition
The Hardware Element UoF provides the capability to specify that an element within a breakdown is hardware and can be associated with the hardware part(s) that fulfill the requirement.

2 HardwareElement

Definition

`HardwareElement` is a `BreakdownElement` that is realized as a
`HardwarePartAsDesigned`.

References

- `BreakdownElement`, refer to Chap 2.2
- `HardwarePartAsDesigned`, refer to Para 8

Type

- UML class

3 HardwareElementPartRealization

Definition

`HardwareElementPartRealization` is a <<relationship>> where a
`HardwareElementRevision` relates to an instance of
`HardwarePartAsDesigned` which fulfills the `HardwareElement` specification.

References

- `HardwareElement`, refer to Para 2
- `HardwareElementRevision`, refer to Para 6
- `HardwarePartAsDesigned`, refer to Para 8

Type

- UML class

4 hardwareElementRepairability

Definition

`hardwareElementRepairability` is a classification that indicates whether the
`HardwareElement` part realization is expected to be repairable from a technical
standpoint, independent of customer maintenance concepts.

Reference

`HardwareElement`, refer to Para 2

Valid values

- R (SX001G:repairableHardwareElement)
- P (SX001G:partialRepairableHardwareElement)
- N (SX001G:nonRepairableHardwareElement)

Type

- CDM `ClassificationType`

5 hardwareElementReplaceability

Definition

`hardwareElementReplaceability` is a classification that identifies whether the
`HardwareElement` part realization is expected to be replaceable from a technical
standpoint, independent from customer maintenance concepts.

Reference

- `HardwareElement`, refer to Para 2

Valid values
- R (SX001G:replaceableHardwareElement)
- N (SX001G:nonReplaceableHardwareElement)

Type
- CDM `ClassificationType`

6 HardwareElementRevision

Definition
`HardwareElementRevision` is a `BreakdownElementRevision` representing an iteration applied to a `HardwareElement`.

References
- `BreakdownElementRevision`, refer to Chap 2.2
- `HardwareElement`, refer to Para 2

Type
- UML class

7 hardwareElementType

Definition
`hardwareElementType` is a classification that identifies further specialization for a `HardwareElement`.

Reference
- `HardwareElement`, refer to Para 2

Valid values
- EQP (SX001G:equipmentHardwareElement)
- PNL (SX001G:panelHardwareElement)
- OPN (SX001G:openingHardwareElement)

Examples
- Panel
- Slot
- Electrical panel
- Equipment
- Access point
- Door

Type
- CDM `ClassificationType`

8 HardwarePartAsDesigned

Definition
`HardwarePartAsDesigned` is a `PartAsDesigned` that is to be realized as physical items, including non-countable material.

Note
Examples of non-countable materials are: oil, sealant, paint.

Reference
- `PartAsDesigned`, refer to Chap 2.16

Type
- UML class

9 HardwarePartAsDesignedDesignData

Definition

`HardwarePartAsDesignedDesignData` is an <<attributeGroup>> that collects `HardwarePartAsDesigned` characteristics identified during design activities.

Reference
- `HardwarePartAsDesigned`, refer to Para 8

Type
- UML class

10 HardwarePartAsDesignedSupportData

Definition

`HardwarePartAsDesignedSupportData` is an <<attributeGroup>> that collects `HardwarePartAsDesigned` characteristics identified during supportability analysis activities.

Reference
- `HardwarePartAsDesigned`, refer to Para 8

Type
- UML class

11 hardwarePartHazardousClass

Definition

`hardwarePartHazardousClass` is a classification that identifies to what extent a `HardwarePartAsDesigned` is capable of posing a significant risk to health, safety or property during transportation, handling or storage.

Reference
- `HardwarePartAsDesigned`, refer to Para 8

Type
- CDM `ClassificationType`

12 hardwarePartLogisticsCategory

Definition

`hardwarePartLogisticsCategory` is a classification that defines the role of the `HardwarePartAsDesigned` in the context of product support.

Reference
- `HardwarePartAsDesigned`, refer to Para 8

Valid values
- R (SX001G:repairableSparePart)
- E (SX001G:expendableSparePart)
- SE (SX001G:supportEquipment)
- C (SX001G:consumablePart)
- M (SX001G:rawMaterial)
- D (SX001G:disposablePart)

- S (SX001G:sparePart)
- HT (SX001G:standardHandTool)
- PE (SX001G:personalProtectionPart)
- EP (SX001G:expendablePersonalProtectionPart)
- PR (SX001G:productProtectionPart)
- PA (SX001G:packagingPart)
- IT (SX001G:informationTechnologyPart)

Type
- CDM ClassificationType

13 hardwarePartOperationalAuthorizedLife

Definition

hardwarePartOperationalAuthorizedLife is an extended property that identifies the maximum usage limit for which an item can be operated, and upon reaching this limit, any further usage of the item must be re-authorized.

Examples
- Hours
- Cycles
- Calendar
- Landings

Type
- CDM AuthorizedLife

14 hardwarePartRepairability

Definition

hardwarePartRepairability is a classification that identifies the extent to which the HardwarePartAsDesigned is repairable from a technical perspective, independent of customer maintenance concepts.

Reference
- HardwarePartAsDesigned, refer to Para 8

Valid values
- R (SX001G:repairablePart)
- P (SX001G:partialRepairablePart)
- N (SX001G:nonRepairablePart)

Type
- CDM ClassificationType

15 hardwarePartScrapRate

Definition

hardwarePartScrapRate is a property that defines the fraction of repairable units which, when removed from service, will be found to be beyond economic repair and therefore have to be scrapped.

Type
- CDM NumericalPropertyType

16   height

Definition

`height` is a property that specifies the vertical longitudinal dimension of an object.

Type

— CDM `PropertyType`

17   hour

Definition

`hour` is an Integer that represents the hour of a day expressed as a value between '0' and '24'.

Reference

— `value`, refer to Chap 2.22

Type

— UML integer

18   hourOffset

Definition

`hourOffset` is an Integer that represents the number of hours by which a time is offset from Coordinated Universal Time expressed as a value between '0' and '14'.

Reference

— `value`, refer to Chap 2.22

Type

— UML integer

Chapter 2.9

Glossary - I

Table of contents

List of tables

References

Table 1 References

Chap No./Document No.	Title
Chap 2.18	Glossary - R
Chap 2.19	Glossary - S
Chap 2.20	Glossary - T

1   IdentifiedTaskRequirement

Definition

`IdentifiedTaskRequirement` is a <<relationship>> that associates a `TaskRequirement` with a `TaskRequirementAnalysisItem`.

References

- `TaskRequirement`, refer to Chap 2.20
- `TaskRequirementAnalysisItem`, refer to Chap 2.20

Type

- UML class

2   identifier

Definition

`identifier` is a string of characters that conveys the identification.

Type

- UML string

3   identifierClassifier

Definition

`identifierClassifier` is a word or a code that determines the meaning of the identifier.

Reference

- `identifier`, refer to Para 2

Examples

- OEM part number
- NCAGE-code

Type

- CDM `validValue`

4   identifierSetBy

Definition

`identifierSetBy` identifies the organization that is responsible for the identifier.

Reference

- `identifier`, refer to Para 2

Type

- CDM `Organization`

5   IdentifierType

Definition

`IdentifierType` is an S-Series IPS specification defined <<primitive>> that represents any kind of identification along with its core characterizations.

Type

- UML class

6   ILS

Definition

Integrated Logistic Support

Reference

- Integrated Logistic Support, refer to Para 39

Type

- Acronym

7   IPC

Definition

Illustrated Parts Catalogue.

Type

- Acronym

8   IPS

Definition

Integrated Product Support.

Reference

- Integrated Product Support, refer to Para 40

Type

- Acronym

9   In Service Optimization Analysis UoF

Definition

The In Service Optimization Analysis UoF provides the capability to represent the result from an actual analysis carried out for the analyzed item and in accordance with a defined decision tree template.

10 ISO

Definition
International Organization for Standardization.

Type
– Acronym

11 individual

Definition
Refer to person.

Reference
– person, refer to Chap 2.16

Type
– Business Term

12 informationCodeVariant

Definition
`informationCodeVariant` is a string of characters that represents the information code variant attribute of the data module code.

Note
An `informationCodeVariant` must be created in accordance with the rules defined in S1000D.

Type
– UML string

13 InfrastructureCompliance

Definition
`InfrastructureCompliance` is a <<relationship>> that documents how the `InfrastructureCompliantItem` fulfills requirements stated in the associated `ResourceSpecification`.

References
– `InfrastructureCompliantItem`, refer to Para 17
– `ResourceSpecification`, refer to Chap 2.18

Type
– UML class

14 infrastructureComplianceDate

Definition
`infrastructureComplianceDate` is a date that defines when infrastructure compliance was declared.

Type
– CDM `DateType`

15 infrastructureComplianceDescription

Definition

`infrastructureComplianceDescription` is a description that gives more information on compliance fulfillment.

Type
- CDM `DescriptorType`

16 infrastructureComplianceLevel

Definition

`infrastructureComplianceLevel` is a classification that specifies the degree of compliance.

Valid values
- P (SX001G:partialInfrastructureCompliance)
- F (SX001G:fullInfrastructureCompliance)
- N (SX001G:nonInfrastructureCompliance)

Type
- CDM `ClassificationType`

17 InfrastructureCompliantItem

Definition

`InfrastructureCompliantItem` is an <<extend>> interface that provides its associated data model to those classes that implement it.

Type
- UML <<extend>> stereotype

18 InServiceOptimizationAnalysis

Definition

`InServiceOptimizationAnalysis` is a <<class>> that represents the result from an in-service optimization analysis carried out for the `InServiceOptimizationAnalysisItem`.

Reference
- `InServiceOptimizationAnalysisItem`, refer to Para 19

Type
- UML class

19 InServiceOptimizationAnalysisItem

Definition

`InServiceOptimizationAnalysisItem` is an <<extend>> interface that provides its associated data model to those classes that can have an associated `InServiceOptimizationAnalysis`.

Reference
- `InServiceOptimizationAnalysis`, refer to Para 18

Type
- UML <<extend>> stereotype

20   inServiceOptimizationAnalysisName

Definition

`inServiceOptimizationAnalysisName` is a name by which the `InServiceOptimizationAnalysis` is known and can be easily referenced.

Reference

- `InServiceOptimizationAnalysis`, refer to Para 18

Type
- CDM NameType

21   inServiceOptimizationAnalysisRationale

Definition

`inServiceOptimizationAnalysisRationale` is a description that gives more information on the reason for the defined `InServiceOptimizationAnalysis`.

Reference

- `InServiceOptimizationAnalysis`, refer to Para 18

Type
- CDM `DescriptorType`

22   InServiceOptimizationAnalysisRevision

Definition

`InServiceOptimizationAnalysisRevision` is a <<class>> representing an iteration applied to an `InServiceOptimizationAnalysis`.

Reference

- `InServiceOptimizationAnalysis`, refer to Para 18

Type
- UML class

23   inServiceOptimizationAnalysisRevisionDate

Definition

`inServiceOptimizationAnalysisRevisionDate` is a date that specifies when an `InServiceOptimizationAnalysis` was revised.

Reference

- `InServiceOptimizationAnalysis`, refer to Para 18

Type
- CDM `DateType`

24   inServiceOptimizationAnalysisRevisionIdentifier

Definition

`inServiceOptimizationAnalysisRevisionIdentifier` is an identifier that establishes a unique designator for an `InServiceOptimizationAnalysisRevision` and to differentiate it from other instances of `InServiceOptimizationAnalysisRevision`.

References
- `InServiceOptimizationAnalysisRevision`, refer to Para 22
- `identifier`, refer to Para 2

Valid values
- ID (SX001G:inServiceOptimizationAnalysisRevisionIdentifier)

Type
- CDM `IdentifierType`

25   inServiceOptimizationAnalysisRevisionRationale

Definition
`inServiceOptimizationAnalysisRevisionRationale` is a description that gives more information on the justification for revising the defined `InServiceOptimizationAnalysis`.

Reference
- `InServiceOptimizationAnalysis`, refer to Para 18

Type
- CDM `DescriptorType`

26   inServiceOptimizationAnalysisRevisionStatus

Definition
`inServiceOptimizationAnalysisRevisionStatus` is a state that identifies the maturity of a `InServiceOptimizationAnalysisRevision`.

References
- `InServiceOptimizationAnalysisRevision`, refer to Para 22
- `state`, refer to Chap 2.19

Type
- CDM `StateType`

27   InServiceOptimizationAnalysisStep

Definition
`InServiceOptimizationAnalysisStep` is a <<class>> that represents the results from an individual step in the associated decision process.

Type
- UML class

28   inServiceOptimizationAnalysisStepDescription

Definition
`inServiceOptimizationAnalysisStepDescription` is a description that gives information on actions taken, information gathered, decisions and conclusions made during the `InServiceOptimizationAnalysisStep`.

Reference
- `InServiceOptimizationAnalysisStep`, refer to Para 27

Type
- CDM DescriptorType

29   inServiceOptimizationAnalysisStepIdentifier

Definition

`inServiceOptimizationAnalysisStepIdentifier` is an identifier that establishes a unique designator for an `InServiceOptimizationAnalysisStep` and to differentiate it from other instances of `InServiceOptimizationAnalysisStep`.

References

- `InServiceOptimizationAnalysisStep`, refer to Para 27
- `identifier`, refer to Para 2

Valid values

- ID (SX001G:inServiceOptimizationAnalysisStepIdentifier)

Type

- CDM `IdentifierType`

30   inServiceOptimizationAnalysisStepQuestionAnswer

Definition

`inServiceOptimizationAnalysisStepQuestionAnswer` is a Boolean that specifies a true or false conclusion to the associated question.

Type

- UML Boolean

31   inServiceOptimizationAnalysisSummaryDescription

Definition

`inServiceOptimizationAnalysisSummaryDescription` is a description that gives summarized information on decisions and conclusions made during the `InServiceOptimizationAnalysis`.

Reference

- `InServiceOptimizationAnalysis`, refer to Para 18

Type

- CDM `DescriptorType`

32   InstallationLocation

Definition

`InstallationLocation` is a <<class>> that represents a position within the associated `SerializedProductVariant`.

Note

`InstallationLocation` is also referred to as installation slot.

Reference

- `SerializedProductVariant`, refer to Chap 2.19

Type

- UML class

33   InstallationLocationDefinitionItem

Definition

`InstallationLocationDefinitionItem` is a <<select>> interface that identifies items which can contain the basic definition for the `InstallationLocation`.

Reference

`InstallationLocation`, refer to <u>Para 32</u>

Type
– UML <<select>> stereotype

34   installationLocationIdentifier

Definition

`installationLocationIdentifier` is an identifier that establishes a unique designator for a `InstallationLocation` and to differentiate it from other instances of `InstallationLocation`.

References
– `InstallationLocation`, refer to <u>Para 32</u>
– `identifier`, refer to <u>Para 2</u>

Valid values
– ID (SX001G:installationLocationIdentifier)

Type
– CDM `IdentifierType`

35   installationLocationName

Definition

`installationLocationName` is a name by which the `InstallationLocation` is known and can be easily referenced.

Reference
– `InstallationLocation`, refer to <u>Para 32</u>

Type
– CDM `NameType`

36   installedDateTime

Definition

`installedDateTime` is a date and time that specifies the exact point in time when the `RealizedPart` was installed at the `InstallationLocation`.

References
– `InstallationLocation`, refer to <u>Para 32</u>
– `RealizedPart`, refer to <u>Chap 2.18</u>

Type
– CDM `DateTimeType`

37 InstalledPart

Definition

`InstalledPart` is a <<class>> that identifies a period during which a given
`RealizedPart` is, or has been, installed at the `InstallationLocation`.

References

- `InstallationLocation`, refer to Para 32
- `RealizedPart`, refer to Chap 2.18

Type

- UML class

38 InstalledPartItem

Definition

`InstalledPartItem` is an <<extend>> interface that provides its associated data model
to those classes that implement it.

Type

- UML <<extend>> stereotype

39 Integrated Logistics Support

Definition

Refer to Integrated Product Support

Note

The term Integrated Logistics Support is replaced with the term Integrated Product Support
(IPS)

Reference

- Integrated Product Support, refer to Para 40

Type

- Business Term

40 Integrated Product Support

Definition

Integrated Product Support is Product support that ensures that all support elements are
considered and harmonized.

Note

Integrated Product Support (IPS) replaces the legacy term Integrated Logistics Support
(ILS)

Reference

- Integrated Logistics Support, refer to Para 39

Type

- Business Term

41 Item

Definition

- an object of attention, concern, or interest (Merriam Webster)
- any level of an assembly (S1000D)
- a thing that is determined or specified (STE-100)

Type
–   Business Term

42   itemLocationCode

Definition

`itemLocationCode` is a string of characters that represents the item location code attribute of the data module code.

Note

An `itemLocationCode` must be created in accordance with the rules defined in S1000D.

Type
–   UML string

Page intentionally blank.

Chapter 2.10

Glossary - J

Table of contents
Page

List of tables

References

Table 1 References

Chap No./Document No.	Title
Chap 2.11	Glossary - K
Chap 2.16	Glossary - P
Chap 2.19	Glossary - S
Chap 2.20	Glossary - T

1 Job

Definition

Job is a term that represents a collection of homogeneous tasks related by similarity of knowledge and skill requirements and can be assigned to a person

Note 1

Many persons can be assigned to the same job

Note 2

a Job can be accomplished, quantified, measured, and rated.

Reference2

- Knowledge, refer to Chap 2.11
- Person, refer to Chap 2.16
- Skill, refer to Chap 2.19
- Task, refer to Chap 2.20
- Term, refer to Chap 2.20

Type

- Business Term

Page intentionally blank.

Chapter 2.11

Glossary - K

Table of contents

Page

List of tables

References

Table 1 References

Chap No./Document No.	Title
Chap 2.16	Glossary - P

1   Knowledge

Definition
Knowledge is a term that represents facts and information acquired by a person.

Note
Refer to skill in terms of the application of knowledge

Reference
– Person, refer to Chap 2.16

Type
– Business Term

Page intentionally blank.

Chapter 2.12

Glossary - L

Table of contents

List of tables

References

Table 1 References

Chap No./Document No.	Title
Chap 2.1	Glossary - A
Chap 2.5	Glossary - E
Chap 2.7	Glossary - G
Chap 2.22	Glossary - V

1 latitude

Definition

`latitude` is a string of characters that contributes to uniquely identifies a `GlobalPosition`.

Reference

`GlobalPosition`, refer to Chap 2.7

Examples
- 39.5693900
- 39°34.1634' N
- 39°34'09" N

Type
- UML string

2 learnCode

Definition

`learnCode` is a string of characters that represents the learn code attribute of the data module code.

Note

A `learnCode` must be created in accordance with the rules defined in S1000D.

Type
- UML string

3 learnEventCode

Definition

`learnEventCode` is a string of characters that represents the learn event code attribute of the data module code.

Note

A `learnEventCode` must be created in accordance with the rules defined in S1000D.

Type
- UML string

4 LegalParty

Definition
`LegalParty` is a <<select>> interface identifies entities that has legal standing in the eyes of the law.

Type
- UML <<select>> stereotype

5 length

Definition
`length` is a property that specifies the most extended longitudinal dimension of an object.

Type
- CDM `PropertyType`

6 lifeAuthorizingOrganization

Definition
`lifeAuthorizingOrganization` identifies the organization that is the authoritative source for the `authorizedLifeValue`.

Reference
- `authorizedLifeValue`, refer to Chap 2.1

Type
- CDM Organization

7 Location

Definition
`Location` is an <<extend>> interface that provides its associated data model to those classes that implement it.

Type
- UML <<extend>> stereotype

8 Location UoF

Definition
The Location UoF provides the capability to define a geographic location.

Reference
- `Location`, refer to Para 7

9 LocationItem

Definition
`LocationItem` is a <<select>> interface that identifies items which can be selected to provide the definition of a geographic location.

Type
- UML <<select>> stereotype

10   LocationRelationship

Definition

`LocationRelationship` is a <<relationship>> where one `LocationItem` relates to another `LocationItem`

Reference

- `LocationItem`, refer to Para 9

Type

- UML class

11   locationRelationshipType

Definition

`locationRelationshipType` is a classification that identifies the meaning of the established relationship.

Valid values

- NXT (SX001G:locationLocatedNextTo)
- IN (SX001G:locationLocatedIn)

Examples

- Located next to
- Located in

Type

- CDM `ClassificationType`

12   LogicalAND

Definition

`LogicalAND` is an `EvaluationCriteria` that defines a Boolean operation where the results of all its associated `EvaluationCriteria` must be TRUE for the result to be TRUE, otherwise the result is FALSE.

Reference

- `EvaluationCriteria`, refer to Chap 2.5

Type

- UML class

13   LogicalNOT

Definition

`LogicalNOT` is an `EvaluationCriteria` that defines a Boolean operation where the result from its associated `EvaluationCriteria` must be FALSE for the result to be TRUE, otherwise the result is FALSE.

Reference

- `EvaluationCriteria`, refer to Chap 2.5

Type

- UML class

14 LogicalOR

Definition

`LogicalOR` is an `EvaluationCriteria` that defines a Boolean operation where the result from at least one of its associated `EvaluationCriteria` must be TRUE for the result to be TRUE, otherwise the result is FALSE.

Reference

- `EvaluationCriteria`, refer to Chap 2.5

Type

- UML class

15 LogicalXOR

Definition

`LogicalXOR` is an `EvaluationCriteria` that defines a Boolean operation where the result from one and only one of its associated `EvaluationCriteria` must be TRUE for the result to be TRUE, otherwise the result is FALSE.

Reference

- `EvaluationCriteria`, refer to Chap 2.5

Type

- UML class

16 longitude

Definition

`longitude` is a string of characters that represents a geographic coordinate specifying the east–west position of a point.

Examples

- 2.6502400°
- 2°39.0144' E
- 2°39'00" E

Type

- UML string

17 lowerBound

Definition

`lowerBound` is a string of characters that represents the lower limit of the range.

Type

- UML string

18 lowerLimitValue

Definition

`lowerLimitValue` is a Real that represents the lower limit of the value range.

Reference

- `value`, refer to Chap 2.22

Type

- UML real

19 lowerOffsetValue

Definition
lowerOffsetValue is a Real that defines the lower limit variation from the nominal value.

Reference
– `value`, refer to Chap 2.22

Type
– UML real

20 LSA

Definition
Logistics Support Analysis.

Type
– Acronym

Chapter 2.13

Glossary - M

Table of contents

List of tables

References

Table 1 References

Chap No./Document No.	Title
Chap 2.1	Glossary - A
Chap 2.2	Glossary - B
Chap 2.6	Glossary - F
Chap 2.8	Glossary - H
Chap 2.9	Glossary - I
Chap 2.16	Glossary - P
Chap 2.19	Glossary - S
Chap 2.22	Glossary - V

1   Maintenance

Definition

Maintenance is an activity that retains or restores a physical item to a specified condition or level of performance.

Reference

– Activity, refer to Chap 2.1
– Item, refer to Chap 2.9

Type

– Business Term

2   MaintenanceFacility

Definition

`MaintenanceFacility` is a Facility that is mainly established for providing product support.

Reference

- `Facility`, refer to Chap 2.6

Type
- UML class

3   maintenanceFacilityType

Definition

`maintenanceFacilityType` is a classification that identifies further specialization for a `MaintenanceFacility`.

Reference

- `MaintenanceFacility`, refer to Para 1

Valid values
- HAN (SX001G:hangar)
- SHOP (SX001G:generalPurposeWorkshop)
- REP (SX001G:repairWorkshop)
- CAL (SX001G:calibrationWorkshop)
- BAT (SX001G:batteryWorkshop)
- HYD (SX001G:hydraulicWorkshop)

Type
- CDM `ClassificationType`

4   MaintenanceLevel

Definition

`MaintenanceLevel` is a <<class>> that represents the definition of a set of maintenance capabilities which will be made available to support a defined `Product`.

Note

`MaintenanceLevel` might be established either by a single organization or be distributed between a set of organizations.

Reference

- `Product`, refer to Chap 2.16

Type
- UML class

5   maintenanceLevelCapabilityDescription

Definition

`maintenanceLevelCapabilityDescription` is a description that gives more information on the ability to perform maintenance based on availability of support resources and environmental conditions.

Note 1

Support resources include eg, personnel and skills, special facilities and support equipment, etc.

Note 2

The defined abilities are the basis for determining the functions to be accomplished at the defined maintenance level.

Type

- CDM `DescriptorType`

6 maintenanceLevelIdentifier

Definition

`maintenanceLevelIdentifier` is an identifier that establishes a unique designator for a MaintenanceLevel and to differentiate it from other instances of `MaintenanceLevel`.

References

- `MaintenanceLevel`, refer to Para 4
- `identifier`, refer to Chap 2.9

Valid values

- ID (SX001G:maintenanceLevelIdentifier)

Type

- CDM `IdentifierType`

7 maintenanceLevelName

Definition

`maintenanceLevelName` is a name by which the `MaintenanceLevel` is known and can be easily referenced.

Reference

- `MaintenanceLevel`, refer to Para 4

Type

- CDM `NameType`

8 maintenanceSignificantOrRelevant

Definition

`maintenanceSignificantOrRelevant` is a classification that identifies whether a `BreakdownElement` requires maintenance activities or not.

Note 1

A maintenance relevant item is an item which can be repaired or replaced as a result of failure or damage.

Note 2

A maintenance significant item is an item which was identified by any selection process coming from a scheduled maintenance analysis like MSG-3 or S4000P. For this type of item, a scheduled maintenance task will be documented.

Reference

- `BreakdownElement`, refer to Chap 2.2

Valid values
- R (SX001G:maintenanceRelevantBreakdownElement)
- S (SX001G:maintenanceSignificantBreakdownElement)
- N (SX001G:nonMaintenanceSignificantOrRelevantBreakdownElement)

Type
- CDM `ClassificationType`

9   materialItemCategoryCode

Definition

`materialItemCategoryCode` is a string of characters that represents the material item category code attribute of the data module code.

Note

A `materialItemCategoryCode` must be created in accordance with the rules defined in S1000D.

Type
- UML string

10   Measurement Point UoF

Definition

The Measurement Point UoF provides the capability to record measured values for its associated item.

11   MeasurementPoint

Definition

`MeasurementPoint` is a <<class>> that represents a measured value recorded for the associated item.

Reference
- `value`, refer to Chap 2.22

Type
- UML class

12   measurementPointIdentifier

Definition

`measurementPointIdentifier` is an identifier that establishes a unique designator for a `MeasurementPoint` and to differentiate it from other instances of `MeasurementPoint`.

References
- `MeasurementPoint`, refer to Para 11
- `identifier`, refer to Chap 2.9

Valid values
- ID (SX001G:measurementPointIdentifier)

Type
- CDM `IdentifierType`

13 MeasurementPointItem

Definition

`MeasurementPointItem` is an <<extend>> interface that provides its associated data model to those classes that implement it.

Type
- UML <<extend>> stereotype

14 measurementPointValue

Definition

`measurementPointValue` is a property that represents the value that is recorded for the `MeasurementPoint`.

References
- `MeasurementPoint`, refer to Para 11
- `value`, refer to Chap 2.22

Type
- CDM `PropertyType`

15 Message

Definition

`Message` is a <<class>> that represents the collection of information brought together by a message sender for the purpose of communicating it to another party.

Type
- UML class

16 Message UoF

Definition

Message UoF provides the capability to identify a collection of information to be communicated from one party to another.

Reference
- Message, refer to Para 15

17 MessageContent

Definition

`MessageContent` is a <<exchange>> definition that represents the collection of information that is the subject of the `Message`.

Reference
- `Message`, refer to Para 15

Type
- UML class

18 messageContentStatus

Definition

`messageContentStatus` is a state that identifies the quality assurance status of the message content.

Reference
- `state`, refer to Chap 2.19

Valid values
- D (SX001G:draftMessageContent)
- F (SX001G:finalMessageContent)
- P (SX001G:preliminaryMessageContent)

Type
- CDM `StateType`

19 messageContentType

Definition
`messageContentType` is a classification that characterizes the information included in the message content.

Valid values
- B (SX001G:baselineMessage)
- U (SX001G:netChangeMessage)

Type
- CDM `ClassificationType`

20 MessageContext

Definition
`MessageContext` is a <<relationship>> between a `Message` and the context for which it is being provided.

Reference
- `Message`, refer to Para 15

Examples
- Product
- Project
- Contract

Type
- UML class

21 MessageContextItem

Definition
`MessageContextItem` is a <<select>> interface that identifies items which can be selected as the context for a `Message`.

Reference
- `Message`, refer to Para 15

Type
- UML <<select>> stereotype

22 messageCreationDateTime

Definition
`messageCreationDateTime` is a date and time that defines when the Message was generated.

Reference
- Message, refer to <u>Para 15</u>

Type
- CDM DateTimeType

23   messageIdentifier

Definition
messageIdentifier is an identifier that establishes a unique designator for a Message and allows it to be differentiated from other instances of Messages.

References
- Message, refer to <u>Para 15</u>
- identifier, refer to <u>Chap 2.9</u>

Valid values
- ID (SX001G:messageIdentifier)

Type
- CDM IdentifierType

24   messageLanguage

Definition
messageLanguage is a classification that identifies the language of the information in the message content.

Type
- CDM ClassificationType

25   MessageParty

Definition
MessageParty is a <<relationship>> between a Message and a stakeholder for the Message.

Reference
- Message, refer to <u>Para 15</u>

Type
- UML class

26   MessagePartyItem

Definition
MessagePartyItem is a <<select>> interface that identifies items which can be selected as the party for a Message.

Reference
- Message, refer to <u>Para 15</u>

Type
- UML <<select>> stereotype

27   messagePartyType

Definition

`messagePartyType` is a classification that identifies the role of the associated Party.

Valid values
- S (SX001G:messageSender)
- R (SX001G:messageReceiver)
- F (SX001G:messageForwarder)

Examples
- Sender
- Receiver

Type
- CDM `ClassificationType`

28   MessageRelationship

Definition

`MessageRelationship` is a <<relationship>> where one `Message` relates to another `Message`.

Reference
- `Message`, refer to Para 15

Examples
- One Message is an update to another Message
- One Message is a reply to another Message

Type
- UML class

29   messageRelationshipType

Definition

`messageRelationshipType` is a classification that characterizes the relationship that is established between two `Messages`.

Valid values
- R (SX001G:replyToMessage)
- A (SX001G:acknowledgementOfMessage)
- U (SX001G:updateToMessage)
- O (SX001G:observationOnMessage)

Type
- CDM `ClassificationType`

30   Military service

Definition

Military service is a term that identifies a distinct branch of armed forces.

Examples
- Army
- Navy
- Air Force

Type
- Business Term

31 minute

Definition
`minute` is an Integer that represents the minute within an hour expressed as a value between '0' and '59'.

References
- `hour`, refer to Chap 2.8
- `value`, refer to Chap 2.22

Type
- UML integer

32 minuteOffset

Definition
`minuteOffset` is an Integer that represents the number of minutes within an hour by which a time is offset from Coordinated Universal Time expressed as either '0', '15', '30' or '45'.

Reference
- `hour`, refer to Chap 2.8

Type
- UML integer

33 Mission Definition UoF

Definition
The Mission Definition UoF supports the definition of operational scenarios to be carried out by a Product.

Reference
- `Product`, refer to Chap 2.16

34 MissionDefinition

Definition
`MissionDefinition` is a <<class>> that represents the defining information for a `Product` operational scenario.

Reference
- `Product`, refer to Chap 2.16

Examples
- Troop transport
- Long haul flight
- Search and rescue

Type
- UML class

35   missionDefinitionDescription

Definition

missionDefinitionDescription is a description of the Product operational scenario.

Reference

-   Product, refer to Chap 2.16

Type

-   CDM DescriptorType

36   missionDefinitionFrequency

Definition

missionDefinitionFrequency is a property that specifies the rate of occurrence.

Type

-   CDM PropertyType

37   MissionDefinitionItem

Definition

MissionDefinitionItem is an <<extend>> interface that provides its associated data model to those classes that implement it.

Type

-   UML <<extend>> stereotype

38   missionDefinitionName

Definition

missionDefinitionName is a name by which the mission definition is known and can be easily referenced.

Type

-   CDM NameType

39   missionDefinitionObjective

Definition

missionDefinitionObjective is a description that specifies the expected end state after the defined MissionDefinition is completed.

References

-   MissionDefinition, refer to Para 34
-   state, refer to Chap 2.19

Type

-   CDM DescriptorType

40   MissionDefinitionParty

Definition

MissionDefinitionParty is a <<relationship>> that establishes an association between a MissionDefinition and a MissionDefinitionPartyItem.

References
- `MissionDefinition`, refer to Para 34
- `MissionDefinitionPartyItem`, refer to Para 41

Type
- UML class

41 MissionDefinitionPartyItem

Definition
`MissionDefinitionPartyItem` is a <<select>> interface that identifies parties which can be associated with a `MissionDefinition`.

Reference
- `MissionDefinition`, refer to Para 34

Type
- UML <<select>> stereotype

42 missionDefinitionPartyRole

Definition
`missionDefinitionPartyRole` is a classification that identifies the association that a `MissionDefinitionParty` has with the `MissionDefinition`.

References
- `MissionDefinition`, refer to Para 34
- `MissionDefinitionParty`, refer to Para 40

Valid values
- C (SX001G:missionDefinitionCarriedOutBy)

Type
- CDM `ClassificationType`

43 MissionDefinitionRelationship

Definition
`MissionDefinitionRelationship` is a <<relationship>> where one `MissionDefinition` relates to another `MissionDefinition`.

Note
Mission definition relationship can be used to represent the relationship between an overarching mission definition and sub-mission definitions.

Reference
- `MissionDefinition`, refer to Para 34

Examples
- Helicopter search and rescue sub-mission definitions for search, locate and rescue, respectively.
- Perform long haul flight sub-mission definitions for takeoff, inflight and land, respectively.

Type
- UML class

44 missionDefinitionRelationshipType

Definition

`missionDefinitionRelationshipType` is a classification that identifies the meaning of the established relationship.

Valid values
- EXT (SX001G:extensionOfMissionDefinition)
- DEP (SX001G:dependentOnMissionDefinition)
- SUB (SX001G:subordinateMissionDefinition)

Type
- CDM `ClassificationType`

45 MissionDefinitionRevision

Definition

`MissionDefinitionRevision` is a <<class>> representing an iteration applied to a `MissionDefinition`.

Reference
- `MissionDefinition`, refer to Para 34

Type
- UML class

46 missionDefinitionRevisionDate

Definition

`missionDefinitionRevisionDate` is a date that specifies when a `MissionDefinition` was revised.

Reference
- `MissionDefinition`, refer to Para 34

Type
- CDM DateType

47 missionDefinitionRevisionIdentifier

Definition

`missionDefinitionRevisionIdentifier` is an identifier that establishes a unique designator for a `MissionDefinitionRevision` and to differentiate it from other instances of `MissionDefinitionRevision`.

References
- `MissionDefinitionRevision`, refer to Para 45
- `identifier`, refer to Chap 2.9

Valid values
- ID (SX001G:missionDefinitionRevisionIdentifier)

Type
- CDM `IdentifierType`

48 missionDefinitionRevisionRationale

Definition

`missionDefinitionRevisionRationale` is a description that gives more information on the justification for revising the `MissionDefinition`.

Reference

- `MissionDefinition`, refer to Para 34

Type

- CDM `DescriptorType`

49 missionDefinitionRevisionStatus

Definition

`missionDefinitionRevisionStatus` is a state that identifies the maturity of a `MissionDefinitionRevision`.

References

- `MissionDefinitionRevision`, refer to Para 45
- `state`, refer to Chap 2.19

Type

- CDM `StateType`

50 missionDefinitionType

Definition

`missionDefinitionType` is a classification that identifies further specialization for a `MissionDefinition`.

Reference

- `MissionDefinition`, refer to Para 34

Valid values

- SAR (SX001G:searchAndRescueMission)
- SRV (SX001G:surveillanceMission)

Type

- CDM `ClassificationType`

51 modelIdentificationCode

Definition

`modelIdentificationCode` is a string of characters that represents the model identification code attribute of the data module code.

Note

A modelIdentificationCode must be created in accordance with the rules defined in S1000D.

Type

- UML string

52 monthComponent

Definition

`monthComponent` is an Integer that represents the month of a year expressed as a value between '1' and '12'.

Reference
- `value`, refer to Chap 2.22

Valid values
- 1 (SX001G:January)
- 2 (SX001G:February)
- 3 (SX001G:March)
- 4 (SX001G:April)
- 5 (SX001G:May)
- 6 (SX001G:June)
- 7 (SX001G:July)
- 8 (SX001G:August)
- 9 (SX001G:September)
- 10 (SX001G:October)
- 11 (SX001G:November)
- 12 (SX001G:December)

Type
- UML integer

53   MOU

Definition
Memorandum of Understanding

Type
- Acronym

Page intentionally blank.

Chapter 2.14

Glossary - N

Table of contents

List of tables

References

Table 1 References

Chap No./Document No.	Title
Chap 2.1	Glossary - A
Chap 2.5	Glossary - E
Chap 2.15	Glossary - O
Chap 2.16	Glossary - P
Chap 2.21	Glossary - U
Chap 2.22	Glossary - V

1   nameLanguage

Definition

nameLanguage is a word or a code that determines the language in which the nameText is written.

Reference
- `nameText`, refer to <u>Para 3</u>

Type
- CDM `validValue`

2 nameProvidedBy

Definition
`nameProvidedBy` identifies the Organization that defined the `nameText`.

References
- `Organization`, refer to <u>Chap 2.15</u>
- `nameText`, refer to <u>Para 3</u>

Type
- CDM `Organization`

3 nameText

Definition
`nameText` is a string of characters that conveys the informal identification.

Type
- UML string

4 NameType

Definition
`NameType` is an S-Series IPS specifications defined <<primitive>> that represents an informal identification.

Type
- UML class

5 NATO

Definition
North Atlantic Treaty Organization

Type
- Acronym

6 NCAGE

Definition
NATO Commercial and Government Entity

Type
- Acronym

7 NestedAllowedProductConfiguration

Definition
`NestedAllowedProductConfiguration` is a <<relationship>> that defines that one `AllowedProductConfiguration` includes a subordinate `AllowedProductConfiguration`.

Reference
- `AllowedProductConfiguration`, refer to Chap 2.1

Type
- UML class

8   NestedProductVariant

Definition
`NestedProductVariant` is a <<relationship>> that defines that one `ProductVariant` includes a subordinate `ProductVariant`.

Reference
- `ProductVariant`, refer to Chap 2.16

Type
- UML class

9   nominalValue

Definition
`nominalValue` is a Real that specifies a single base value for the specified range.

Reference
- `value`, refer to Chap 2.22

Type
- UML real

10   NonConformanceData

Definition
`NonConformanceData` is an <<attributeGroup>> that collects information on how the `EffectiveOnProductConfigurationItem` does not comply with the requirements of its usage.

Reference
- `EffectiveOnProductConfigurationItem`, refer to Chap 2.5

Type
- UML class

11   nonConformanceDescription

Definition
`nonConformanceDescription` is a description that gives more information on how the `EffectiveOnProductConfigurationItem` does not comply with its requirements.

Reference
- `EffectiveOnProductConfigurationItem`, refer to Chap 2.5

Type
- CDM `DescriptorType`

12   nonConformanceRestriction

Definition

`nonConformanceRestriction` is a description that gives more information on how the use of the related `EffectiveOnProductConfigurationItem` restricts the specified capabilities of the `AllowedProductConfiguration` in which it is contained.

References
- `AllowedProductConfiguration`, refer to Chap 2.1
- `EffectiveOnProductConfigurationItem`, refer to Chap 2.5

Type
- CDM `DescriptorType`

13   nonConformanceType

Definition

`nonConformanceType` is a classification that identifies in which way the `EffectiveOnProductConfigurationItem` does not comply with its requirements.

Reference
- `EffectiveOnProductConfigurationItem`, refer to Chap 2.5

Valid values
- C (SX001G:concession)
- W (SX001G:waiver)

Type
- CDM `ClassificationType`

14   NumericalPropertyType

Definition

`NumericalPropertyType` is a `PropertyType` that represents a quantity by its numerical value together with the unit in which the value is given.

References
- `PropertyType`, refer to Chap 2.16
- `unit`, refer to Chap 2.21
- `value`, refer to Chap 2.22

Type
- UML class

Chapter 2.15

Glossary - O

Table of contents

List of tables

References

Table 1 References

Chap No./Document No.	Title
Chap 2.6	Glossary - F
Chap 2.9	Glossary - I
Chap 2.16	Glossary - P
Chap 2.20	Glossary - T

1   OASIS

Definition
Organization for the Advancement of Structured Information Standards

Type
–   Acronym

2 OEM

Definition
Original Equipment Manufacturer

References
- Acronym, refer to Para 11

Type
- Acronym

3 Occupational background

Definition
Occupational background is a term that represents the job history which the target audience has in relation to a chosen assignment.

Reference
- Term, refer to Chap 2.20

Type
- Business Term

4 OperatingBase

Definition
OperatingBase is a Facility that is mainly established for providing support for operations.

Reference
- Facility, refer to Chap 2.6

Examples
- harbor
- garage
- airfield

Type
- UML class

5 operatingBaseType

Definition
operatingBaseType is a classification that identifies further specialization for a OperatingBase.

Reference
- OperatingBase, refer to Para 4

Valid values
- F (SX001G:forwardOperatingBase)
- M (SX001G:mainOperatingBase)
- D (SX001G:deploymentOperatingBase)

Type
- CDM ClassificationType

6   OperatingLocationType

Definition

OperatingLocationType is a <<class>> that represents the definition of the nature of the environment in which a product will be operated.

Type
- UML class

7   operatingLocationTypeDescription

Definition

operatingLocationTypeDescription is a description that gives more information on the OperatingLocationType, including the environmental conditions to be expected.

Reference
- OperatingLocationType, refer to Para 6

Type
- CDM DescriptorType

8   operatingLocationTypeIdentifier

Definition

operatingLocationTypeIdentifier is an identifier that establishes a unique designator for an OperatingLocationType and to differentiate it from other instances of OperatingLocationType.

References
- OperatingLocationType, refer to Para 6
- identifier, refer to Chap 2.9

Valid values
- ID (SX001G:operatingLocationTypeIdentifier)

Type
- CDM IdentifierType

9   operatingLocationTypeName

Definition

operatingLocationTypeName is a name by which the OperatingLocationType is known and can be easily referenced.

Reference
- OperatingLocationType, refer to Para 6

Type
- CDM NameType

10   OperationalTask

Definition

OperationalTask is a Task that is required to support the use of a product.

Reference
- Task, refer to Chap 2.20

Examples
- Fueling
- Towing

Type
- UML class

11 Original equipment manufacturer

Definition
Original equipment manufacturer is an organization that owns the design and manufacturing rights for a part.

References
- Organization, refer to Para 12
- PartAsDesigned, refer to Chap 2.16

Type
- Business Term

12 Organization

Definition
Organization is a <<class>> that represents an administrative structure with a particular purpose belonging to a legal entity.

Examples
- International agency
- Government department
- Company
- Department

Type
- UML class

13 Organization UoF

Definition
The Organization UoF provides the capability to identify organizations.

Reference
- Organization, refer to Para 11

14 organizationIdentifier

Definition
organizationIdentifier is an identifier that establishes a unique designator for an Organization and allows it to be differentiated from other instances of Organization.

References
- Organization, refer to Para 11
- identifier, refer to Chap 2.9

Valid values
- CAGE (SX001G:natoCommercialAndGovernmentEntity)
- ID (SX001G:organizationIdentifier)

Type
- CDM IdentifierType

15 organizationName

Definition

organizationName is a name by which the Organization is known and can be easily referenced.

Reference
- Organization, refer to Para 11

Type
- CDM NameType

Page intentionally blank.

Chapter 2.16

Glossary - P

Table of contents

List of tables

References

Table 1 References

Chap No./Document No.	Title
Chap 2.1	Glossary - A
Chap 2.3	Glossary - C
Chap 2.9	Glossary - I
Chap 2.19	Glossary - S
Chap 2.20	Glossary - T
Chap 2.22	Glossary - V

1   Party

Definition

Party is a term that identifies one side involved in a formal agreement or activity.

Note

A party can be an agent, a person or an organization.

Reference

– Term, refer to Chap 2.20

Examples

– Buyer
– Seller
– Manufacturer
– Contractor

Type

– Business Term

2   packagedTask

Definition

`packagedTask` is a Boolean that specifies if the `Task` is created in order to group a set of defined Tasks for a specific purpose.

Note

Grouping of Tasks that can be performed to support maintenance planning and scheduling activities

Reference

– `Task`, refer to Chap 2.20

Example

– 1000 Flight Hours Overhaul

Type

– UML Boolean

3 ParameterThresholdDefinition

Definition

`ParameterThresholdDefinition` is a `ThresholdDefinition` that is continuously measured and evaluated, and when reached, activates the associated trigger threshold.

Reference

- `ThresholdDefinition`, refer to Chap 2.20

Type

- UML class

4 Part As Realized UoF

Definition

The Part As Realized UoF provides the capability to identify actual existing parts.

5 Part Definition UoF

Definition

The Part Definition UoF provides the capability of defining hardware and software parts, their characteristics, and associated parts lists.

6 PartAsDesigned

Definition

`PartAsDesigned` is a <<class>> that represents the definitional information for an artifact fulfilling a set of requirements, which can be produced or realized.

Type

- UML class

7 PartAsDesignedPartsList

Definition

`PartAsDesignedPartsList` is a <<class>> that represents the definitional information for the collection of `PartAsDesignedPartsListEntry` included in the assembly of the parent `PartAsDesigned`.

Note

`PartAsDesignedPartsList` is typically referred to as a Bill of Material (BOM).

References

- `PartAsDesigned`, refer to Para 6
- `PartAsDesignedPartsListEntry`, refer to Para 8
- `assembly`, refer to Chap 2.1

Type

- UML class

8 PartAsDesignedPartsListEntry

Definition

`PartAsDesignedPartsListEntry` is a <<class>> that represents the inclusion of a `PartAsDesigned` in a `PartAsDesignedPartsListRevision`.

References
- `PartAsDesigned`, refer to Para 6
- `PartAsDesignedPartsListRevision`, refer to Para 11

Type
- UML class

9 PartAsDesignedPartsListRelationship

Definition
`PartAsDesignedPartsListRelationship` is a <<relationship>> where one `PartAsDesignedPartsList` relates to another `PartAsDesignedPartsList`.

Reference
- `PartAsDesignedPartsList`, refer to Para 7

Type
- UML class

10 partAsDesignedPartsListRelationshipType

Definition
`partAsDesignedPartsListRelationshipType` is a classification that identifies the meaning of the established relationship.

Valid values
- C (SX001G:correspondsToPartsList)
- D (SX001G:derivedFromPartsList)
- E (SX001G:extendsPartsList)

Type
- CDM `ClassificationType`

11 PartAsDesignedPartsListRevision

Definition
`PartAsDesignedPartsListRevision` is a <<class>> representing an iteration applied to a `PartAsDesignedPartsList`.

Reference
- `PartAsDesignedPartsList`, refer to Para 7

Type
- UML class

12 partDefinitionIdentifier

Definition
`partDefinitionIdentifier` is an identifier that identifies the design standard to which the serialized part adheres.

Reference
- `identifier`, refer to Chap 2.9

Valid values
- ID (SX001G:partDefinitionIdentifier)
- OEM (SX001G:originalEquipmentManufacturerPartNumber)

- REF (SX001G:partReferenceNumber)
- SUP (SX001G:supplierPartNumber)
- NSN (SX001G:natoStockNumber)
- STD (SX001G:standardsReferenceDesignator)

Type
- CDM IdentifierType

13   partIdentifier

Definition

partIdentifier is an identifier that establishes a unique designator for a PartAsDesigned and to differentiate it from other instances of PartAsDesigned.

Note

Part identification includes drawing, model, type or source controlling numbers.

References
- PartAsDesigned, refer to Para 6
- identifier, refer to Chap 2.9

Valid values
- ID (SX001G:partIdentifier)
- OEM (SX001G:originalEquipmentManufacturerPartNumber)
- REF (SX001G:partReferenceNumber)
- SUP (SX001G:supplierPartNumber)
- STD (SX001G:standardsReferenceDesignator)

Example
- "12345-501"

Type
- CDM IdentifierType

14   partName

Definition

partName is a name by which the PartAsDesigned is known and can be easily referenced.

Reference
- PartAsDesigned, refer to Para 6

Type
- CDM NameType

15   partsListEntryIdentifier

Definition

partsListEntryIdentifier is an identifier that establishes a unique designator for a PartAsDesignedPartsListEntry and to differentiate it from other instances of PartAsDesignedPartsListEntry.

References
- PartAsDesignedPartsListEntry, refer to Para 8
- identifier, refer to Chap 2.9

Valid values
- ID (SX001G:partsListEntryIdentifier)
- LN (SX001G:partsListLineNumber)

Type
- CDM `IdentifierType`

16 partsListEntryQuantity

Definition
`partsListEntryQuantity` is a property that specifies the amount of the `PartAsDesigned` used in its parent `PartAsDesignedPartsListRevision`.

References
- `PartAsDesigned`, refer to Para 6
- `PartAsDesignedPartsListRevision`, refer to Para 11

Type
- CDM `PropertyType`

17 partsListRevisionDate

Definition
`partsListRevisionDate` is a date that specifies when the `PartAsDesignedPartsList` was revised.

Reference
- `PartAsDesignedPartsList`, refer to Para 7

Type
- CDM `DateType`

18 partsListRevisionIdentifier

Definition
`partsListRevisionIdentifier` is an identifier that establishes a unique designator for a `PartAsDesignedPartsListRevision` and to differentiate it from other instances of `PartAsDesignedPartsListRevision` for the same `partsListType`.

References
- `PartAsDesignedPartsListRevision`, refer to Para 11
- `identifier`, refer to Chap 2.9
- `partsListType`, refer to Para 21

Valid values
- ID (SX001G:partsListRevisionIdentifier)

Type
- CDM `IdentifierType`

19 partsListRevisionRationale

Definition
`partsListRevisionRationale` is a description that gives more information on the justification for revising the `PartAsDesignedPartsList`.

Reference
- `PartAsDesignedPartsList`, refer to Para 7

Type
- CDM `DescriptorType`

20 partsListRevisionStatus

Definition
`partsListRevisionStatus` is a state that identifies the maturity of a `PartAsDesignedPartsListRevision`.

References
- `PartAsDesignedPartsListRevision`, refer to Para 11
- `state`, refer to Chap 2.19

Type
- CDM `StateType`

21 partsListType

Definition
`partsListType` is a classification that identifies the context and intended use of the `PartAsDesignedPartsList`.

Reference
- `PartAsDesignedPartsList`, refer to Para 7

Valid values
- PBOM (SX001G:provisioningPartsList)
- EBOM (SX001G:engineeringPartsList)
- SBOM (SX001G:supportPartsList)
- MBOM (SX001G:manufacturingPartsList)

Type
- CDM `ClassificationType`

22 Performance Parameter UoF

Definition
The Performance Parameter UoF supports the definition of metrics that if changed will have a major impact on the system performance, schedule, cost and/or risk.

Reference
- `system`, refer to Chap 2.19

23 PerformanceParameter

Definition
`PerformanceParameter` is a <<class>> that represents a metric that if changed, or not fulfilled, can have a major impact on the performance, schedule, cost and/or risk for the `PerformanceParameterItem`.

Reference
- `PerformanceParameterItem`, refer to Para 25

Type
- UML class

24 performanceParameterCalculationMethod

Definition

performanceParameterCalculationMethod is a description that gives more information on the method by which the performanceParameterValue has been derived.

Reference
- performanceParameterValue, refer to Para 32

Type
- CDM DescriptorType

25 PerformanceParameterItem

Definition

PerformanceParameterItem is an <<extend>> interface that provides its associated data model to those classes that can have an associated PerformanceParameter.

Reference
- PerformanceParameter, refer to Para 23

Type
- UML <<extend>> stereotype

26 PerformanceParameterRevision

Definition

PerformanceParameterRevision is a <<class>> that represents an iteration applied to a PerformanceParameter.

Reference
- PerformanceParameter, refer to Para 23

Type
- UML class

27 performanceParameterRevisionDate

Definition

performanceParameterRevisionDate is a date that defines when a PerformanceParameterRevision was defined.

Reference
- PerformanceParameterRevision, refer to Para 26

Type
- CDM DateType

28   performanceParameterRevisionIdentifier

Definition

`performanceParameterRevisionIdentifier` is an identifier that establishes a unique designator for a `PerformanceParameterRevision` and to differentiate it from other instances of `PerformanceParameterRevision`.

References

- `PerformanceParameterRevision`, refer to Para 26
- `identifier`, refer to Chap 2.9

Valid values

- ID (SX001G:performanceParameterRevisionIdentifier)

Type

- CDM `IdentifierType`

29   performanceParameterRevisionRationale

Definition

`performanceParameterRevisionRationale` is a description that gives more information on the justification for revising the defined `PerformanceParameter` and its values.

Reference

- `PerformanceParameter`, refer to Para 23

Type

- CDM `DescriptorType`

30   performanceParameterRevisionStatus

Definition

`performanceParameterRevisionStatus` is a state that identifies the maturity of a `PerformanceParameterRevision`.

References

- `PerformanceParameterRevision`, refer to Para 26
- `state`, refer to Chap 2.19

Type

- CDM `StateType`

31   performanceParameterType

Definition

`performanceParameterType` is a classification that identifies the type of `PerformanceParameter` being exchanged.

Reference

- `PerformanceParameter`, refer to Para 23

Valid values

- MTBF (SX001G:meanTimeBetweenFailurePerformanceParameter)
- LCC (SX001G:lifeCycleCostPerformanceParameter)
- FR (SX001G:failureRatePerformanceParameter)

- PSL (SX001G:productServiceLifePerformanceParameter)
- SMI (SX001G:scheduledMaintenanceIntervalPerformanceParameter)
- MFOP (SX001G:maintenanceFreeOperatingPeriodPerformanceParameter)
- MDT (SX001G:meanDownTimePerformanceParameter)
- MMHOH (SX001G:maintenanceManHoursPerOperatingHourPerformanceParameter)
- MTBUR (SX001G:meanTimeBetweenUnscheduledRemovalPerformanceParameter)
- MTTR (SX001G:meanTimeToRepairPerformanceParameter)
- DMC (SX001G:directMaintenanceCostPerformanceParameter)
- SPT (SX001G:shopProcessingTimePerformanceParameter)
- FOH (SX001G:failuresPerOperatingHourPerformanceParameter)
- RT (SX001G:replacementTimePerformanceParameter)
- AO (SX001G:operationalAvailabilityPerformanceParameter)
- AF (SX001G:maintenanceFacilityAvailabilityPerformanceParameter)
- AM (SX001G:materialAvailabilityPerformanceParameter)
- AP (SX001G:personnelAvailabilityPerformanceParameter)
- AS (SX001G:sparesIAvailabilityPerformanceParameter)
- ASE (SX001G:supportEquipmentAvailabilityPerformanceParameter)
- CWT (SX001G:customerWaitTimePerformanceParameter)
- MC (SX001G:missionCapableRatePerformanceParameter)
- NMC (SX001G:nonIMissionCapableRatePerformanceParameter)
- PMC (SX001G:partialMissionCapableRatePerformanceParameter)
- MISR (SX001G:missionReliabilityPerformanceParameter)
- MR (SX001G:materialReadinessPerformanceParameter)
- MTTF (SX001G:meanTimeToFailurePerformanceParameter)
- OEE (SX001G:overallEquipmentEffectivenessPerformanceParameter)
- OSC (SX001G:operatingAndSupportCostPerformanceParameter)
- PME (SX001G:preventiveMaintenanceEffectivenessPerformanceParameter)
- PMP (SX001G:plannedMaintenancePercentagePerformanceParameter)
- SE (SX001G:supplyEffectivenesssPerformanceParameter)
- TE (SX001G:trainingEffectivenessPerformanceParameter)
- TSHIP (SX001G:shippingTimePerformanceParameter)

Type
- CDM ClassificationType

32 performanceParameterValue

Definition

`performanceParameterValue` is a property that represents a value which is
determined for the `PerformanceParameter`.

References
- `PerformanceParameter`, refer to Para 23
- `value`, refer to Chap 2.22

Type
- CDM `PropertyType`

33 performanceParameterValueFraction

Definition

`performanceParameterValueFraction` is a property that represents the fraction
of all occurrences related to a specified PerformanceParameter that must be within the limit of
the defined `performanceParameterValue`.

References
- `PerformanceParameter`, refer to Para 23
- `performanceParameterValue`, refer to Para 32

Example
- A customer requirement is that 98% of all replacement tasks must be performed below a specified value of two hours (= maximum replacement time)

Type
- CDM `PropertyType`

34 PerformanceParameterValueGroup

Definition
`PerformanceParameterValueGroup` is an <<attributeGroup>> that organizes `PerformanceParameter` values for a defined purpose.

Reference
- `PerformanceParameter`, refer to Para 23

Type
- UML class

35 performanceParameterValueLimitQualifier

Definition
`performanceParameterValueLimitQualifier` is a classification that specifies a directed limit to be applied when testing a value against the defined `PerformanceParameter`.

References
- `PerformanceParameter`, refer to Para 23
- `value`, refer to Chap 2.22

Valid values
- MAX (SX001G:maximumValueLimitQualifier)
- MIN (SX001G:minimumValueLimitQualifier)

Type
- CDM `ClassificationType`

36 PeriodicTimeLimit

Definition
`PeriodicTimeLimit` is a `TimeLimit` that is repeated and its next occurrence can be scheduled.

Reference
- `TimeLimit`, refer to Chap 2.20

Type
- UML class

37 Person

Definition
Person is a living human being.

Type
- Business Term

38   PlannedTaskItem

Definition

`PlannedTaskItem` is a <<select>> interface that identifies items which can be used in the context of PlannedTaskUsage.

Reference
- `PlannedTaskUsage`, refer to Para 39

Type
- UML <<select>> stereotype

39   PlannedTaskUsage

Definition

`PlannedTaskUsage` is a `TaskUsage` that expands the definition of a required `Task` in the context of a given support solution.

Note

Both rectifying and operational tasks are justified by task requirements identified during various analysis activities.

References
- `Task`, refer to Chap 2.20
- `TaskUsage`, refer to Chap 2.20

Type
- UML class

40   PLCS

Definition

Product Life Cycle Support

Type
- Acronym

41   postalCode

Definition

`postalcode` is a string of characters that represents a short code used by the postal service to identify a geographical area.

Type
- UML string

42   Product and Project UoF

Definition

The Product and Project UoF defines the Product(s) which are in focus for the Integrated Product Support (ILP) analysis activities together with information for the overall IPS project.

References
- `Product`, refer to Para 44
- `Project`, refer to Para 62

43   Product Design Configuration UoF

Definition

The Product Design Configuration UoF defines permitted combinations of breakdown elements, hardware and software, in the context of product variants and allowed product configurations.

Reference

- Product, refer to Para 44

44   Product

Definition

Product is a <<class>> that represents a family of items which share the same underlying design purpose.

Examples

- iPhone 7
- Pegasus engine
- Aegis Class Destroyer
- Stryker
- Ford Fusion
- Airbus A340

Type

- UML class

45   Product support

Definition

Product support is an activity that develops, enables, executes and maintains a sustainment strategy for the Product.

Reference

- Product, refer to Para 44

Type

- Business Term

46   Product Usage Context UoF

Definition

The Product Usage Context UoF defines the context in which the defined Product(s) and Product variant(s) are to be operated and maintained.

Reference

- Product, refer to Para 44

47   Product Usage Phase UoF

Definition

The Product Usage Phase UoF defines periods of time during which a Product is in an operational state which has specific characteristics that need special considerations.

References

- Product, refer to Para 44
- state, refer to Chap 2.19

48 productDefinitionIdentifier

Definition

productDefinitionIdentifier is an identifier that identifies the Product of which the serialized product variant is a realization.

References

- Product, refer to Para 44
- identifier, refer to Chap 2.9

Valid values

- ID (SX001G:productDefinitionIdentifier)
- MOI (SX001G:modelIdentificationCode)
- EIAC (SX001G:endItemAcronymCode)

Type

- CDM IdentifierType

49 productIdentifier

Definition

productIdentifier is an identifier that establishes a unique designator for a Product and to differentiate it from other instances of Product.

References

- Product, refer to Para 44
- identifier, refer to Chap 2.9

Valid values

- ID (SX001G:productIdentifier)
- MOI (SX001G:modelIdentificationCode)
- EIAC (SX001G:endItemAcronymCode)

Type

- CDM IdentifierType

50 productName

Definition

productName is a name by which the Product is known and can be easily referenced.

Reference

- Product, refer to Para 44

Type

- CDM NameType

51 ProductUsagePhase

Definition

ProductUsagePhase is a <<class>> that represents a distinct period of time during which a ProductUsagePhaseItem is in an operational state which has specific characteristics that need special considerations.

References

- ProductUsagePhaseItem, refer to Para 54
- state, refer to Chap 2.19

Examples
- Preflight, post-flight, cruise, taxiing for an aircraft.
- Emersion, surface and dock for a submarine.

Type
- UML class

52 productUsagePhaseDescription

Definition
productUsagePhaseDescription is a description that gives more information on the ProductUsagePhase.

Reference
ProductUsagePhase, refer to Para 51

Type
- CDM DescriptorType

53 productUsagePhaseDuration

Definition
productUsagePhaseDuration is a property that specifies the average time that the ProductUsagePhaseItem will remain in the specified state.

References
- ProductUsagePhaseItem, refer to Para 54
- state, refer to Chap 2.19

Type
- CDM PropertyType

54 ProductUsagePhaseItem

Definition
ProductUsagePhaseItem is an <<extend>> interface that provides its associated data model to those classes that implement it.

Type
- UML <<extend>> stereotype

55 productUsagePhaseName

Definition
productUsagePhaseName is a name by which the ProductUsagePhase is known and can be easily referenced.

Reference
- ProductUsagePhase, refer to Para 51

Type
- CDM NameType

56   ProductUsagePhaseRelationship

Definition

`ProductUsagePhaseRelationship` is a <<relationship>> where one `ProductUsagePhase` relates to another `ProductUsagePhase`.

Reference

- `ProductUsagePhase`, refer to Para 51

Type

- UML class

57   productUsagePhaseRelationshipType

Definition

`productUsagePhaseRelationshipType` is a classification that identifies the meaning of the established relationship.

Valid values

- B (SX001G:happensBeforeProductUsagePhase)
- A (SX001G:happensAfterProductUsagePhase)
- P (SX001G:partOfProductUsagePhase)
- D (SX001G:happensDuringProductUsagePhase)

Type

- CDM `ClassificationType`

58   ProductVariant

Definition

`ProductVariant` is a <<class>> that defines a member of a Product family which is configured for a specific purpose and is made available to the market.

Note

A product variant is often known as a model.

Reference

- `Product`, refer to Para 44

Examples

- Boeing 787-800 vs 787-900
- Ford Fusion S vs. SE vs. SEL

Type

- UML class

59   productVariantDefinitionIdentifier

Definition

`productVariantDefinitionIdentifier` is an identifier that identifies the `Product` variant of which the serialized product variant is a realization.

References

- `Product`, refer to Para 44
- `identifier`, refer to Chap 2.9

Valid values

- ID (SX001G:productVariantDefinitionIdentifier)

- MOI (SX001G:modelIdentificationCode)
- MOV (SX001G:modelVersionIdentifier)
- UOC (SX001G:usableOnCode)

Type
- CDM IdentifierType

60   productVariantIdentifier

Definition

productVariantIdentifier is an identifier that establishes a unique designator for a ProductVariant and to differentiate it from other instances of ProductVariant.

References
- ProductVariant, refer to Para 58
- identifier, refer to Chap 2.9

Valid values
- ID (SX001G:productVariantIdentifier)
- MOI (SX001G:modelIdentificationCode)
- UOC (SX001G:usableOnCode)
- MOV (SX001G:modelVersionIdentifier)

Type
- CDM IdentifierType

61   productVariantName

Definition

productVariantName is a name by which the ProductVariant is known and can be easily referenced.

Reference
- ProductVariant, refer to Para 58

Type
- CDM NameType

62   Project

Definition

Project is a <<class>> that represents the overall set of Integrated Product Support (IPS) activities defined for a Product.

Note

Project is often referred to as an IPS program.

Reference
- Product, refer to Para 44

Type
- UML class

63   ProjectContract

Definition

`ProjectContract` is a <<relationship>> that establishes an association between a `Project` and a Contract.

References

- `Contract`, refer to Chap 2.3
- `Project`, refer to Para 62

Type

- UML class

64   projectIdentifier

Definition

`projectIdentifier` is an identifier that establishes a unique designator for a `Project` and to differentiate it from other instances of `Project`.

References

- `Project`, refer to Para 62
- `identifier`, refer to Chap 2.9

Valid values

- ID (SX001G:projectIdentifier)
- MOI (SX001G:modelIdentificationCode)

Type

- CDM `IdentifierType`

65   projectName

Definition

`projectName` is a name by which the `Project` is known and can be easily referenced.

Reference

- `Project`, refer to Para 62

Type

- CDM `NameType`

66   ProjectSpecificAttribute

Definition

`ProjectSpecificAttribute` is a <<class>> that allows for the definition of an attribute that is specific to a `Project`.

Reference

- `Project`, refer to Para 62

Type

- UML class

67   projectSpecificAttributeName

Definition

`projectSpecificAttributeName` is a valid value that uniquely identifies a `ProjectSpecificAttribute`.

References
- `ProjectSpecificAttribute`, refer to Para 66
- `value`, refer to Chap 2.22

Type
- CDM `validValue`

68   ProjectSpecificAttributeValue

Definition

`ProjectSpecificAttributeValue` is a <<select>> interface that allows to associate an attribute type to a `ProjectSpecificAttribute`.

Reference
- `ProjectSpecificAttribute`, refer to Para 66

Type
- UML <<select>> stereotype

69   ProjectSpecificExtensionItem

Definition

`ProjectSpecificExtensionItem` is an <<extend>> interface that allows to associate one or several `ProjectSpecificAttributes` to any <<class>>.

Type
- UML <<extend>> stereotype

70   PropertyType

Definition

`PropertyType` is an S-Series IPS specifications defined <<primitive>> that represents a measurable characteristic.

Type
- UML class

71   proposedTrainingMethod

Definition

`proposedTrainingMethod` is a classification that suggests the way in which the additional learning can be acquired.

Valid values
- OTJ (SX001G:onTheJobTrainingMethod)
- CR (SX001G:classroomTrainingMethod)
- CW (SX001G:coursewareTrainingMethod)

Type
- CDM `ClassificationType`

72 publicationModuleIssueInWorkNumber

Definition

`publicationModuleIssueInWorkNumber` is a string of characters used for monitoring and control of intermediate drafts of S1000DPublicationModuleIssue.

Note

A `publicationModuleIssueInWorkNumber` must be created in accordance with the rules defined in S1000D.

Reference

- `S1000DPublicationModuleIssue`, refer to Chap 2.19

Type

- UML string

73 publicationModuleIssueLanguage

Definition

`publicationModuleIssueLanguage` is a classification that identifies the language used to produce the content of the `S1000DPublicationModuleIssue`.

Note

A `publicationModuleIssueLanguage` must be created in accordance with the rules defined in S1000D.

Reference

- S1000DPublicationModuleIssue, refer to Chap 2.19

Type

- CDM `ClassificationType`

74 publicationModuleIssueLanguageCountry

Definition

`publicationModuleIssueLanguageCountry` is a classification that identifies the country where the language, identified by `publicationModuleIssueLanguage`, is spoken

Note

A `publicationModuleIssueLanguageCountry` must be created in accordance with the rules defined in S1000D.

Reference

- `publicationModuleIssueLanguage`, refer to Para 73

Type

- CDM `ClassificationType`

75 publicationModuleIssueNumber

Definition

`publicationModuleIssueNumber` is a string of characters used to identify the release number of the S1000DPublicationModuleIssue.

Note

A `publicationModuleIssueNumber` must be created in accordance with the rules defined in S1000D.

Reference
-   S1000DPublicationModuleIssue, refer to Chap 2.19

Type
-   UML string

76   publicationModuleIssuer

Definition
publicationModuleIssuer is a string of characters that represents the issuing
authority attribute of the publication module code.

Note
A publicationModuleIssuer must be created in accordance with the rules
defined in S1000D.

Type
-   UML string

77   publicationModuleNumber

Definition
publicationModuleNumber is a string of characters that represents the number of the
publication module attribute of the publication module code.

Note
A publicationModuleNumber must be created in accordance with the rules
defined in S1000D.

Type
-   UML string

78   publicationModuleVolume

Definition
publicationModuleVolume is a string of characters that represents the volume of the
publication attribute of the publication module code.

Note
A publicationModuleVolume must be created in accordance with the rules
defined in S1000D.

Type
-   UML string

Chapter 2.17

Glossary - Q

Table of contents

List of tables

References

Table 1 References

Chap No./Document No.	Title
Chap 2.4	Glossary - D
Chap 2.8	Glossary - H
Chap 2.9	Glossary - I

1   quantityOfContainedSubstance

Definition

quantityOfContainedSubstance is a property that identifies the amount of the substance included in the HardwarePartAsDesigned.

Reference

−   HardwarePartAsDesigned, refer to Chap 2.8

Type

−   CDM PropertyType

2   QuestionInServiceOptimizationAnalysisStep

Definition

QuestionInServiceOptimizationAnalysisStep is an InServiceOptimizationAnalysisStep that specifies the answer to a question defined in the associated DecisionTreeTemplate.

References

−   DecisionTreeTemplate, refer to Chap 2.4
−   InServiceOptimizationAnalysisStep, refer to Chap 2.9

Type

−   UML class

Page intentionally blank.

Chapter 2.18

Glossary - R

Table of contents
Page

List of tables

References

Table 1 References

Chap No./Document No.	Title
Chap 2.4	Glossary - D
Chap 2.9	Glossary - I
Chap 2.16	Glossary - P
Chap 2.19	Glossary - S
Chap 2.20	Glossary - T

1 RealizedPart

Definition

`RealizedPart` is a <<select>> interface that identifies which items can be used as an `InstalledPart`.

Reference

- `InstalledPart`, refer to Chap 2.9

Type

- UML <<select>> stereotype

2 RectifyingTask

Definition

`RectifyingTask` is a `Task` that ensures or returns the function of the associated item.

Note

An event that can require a `Task` to be performed includes a failure, a damage, a special event and a time limit.

Reference

- `Task`, refer to Chap 2.20

Examples

- Replace
- Repair
- Lubrication

Type

- UML class

3 ReferencedDigitalFile

Definition

`ReferencedDigitalFile` is a <<relationship> that allows an item to refer to a `DigitalFile`.

Reference

- `DigitalFile`, refer to Chap 2.4

Type
- UML class

4   referencedDigitalFileJustification

Definition

`referencedDigitalFileJustification` is a phrase that provides more on information on the reason why the `DigitalFile` is referenced.

Reference
- `DigitalFile`, refer to Chap 2.4

Example
- A video showing the task execution.

Type
- CDM `DescriptorType`

5   ReferencedDocument

Definition

`ReferencedDocument` is a <<relationship>> where one `DocumentReferencingItem` relates to a `DocumentItem`.

References
- `DocumentItem`, refer to Chap 2.4
- `DocumentReferencingItem`, refer to Chap 2.4

Type
- UML class

6   referencedDocumentPortion

Definition

`referencedDocumentPortion` is a description that provides a reference to the portion of a document which is of interest in a specific usage.

Type
- CDM `DescriptorType`

7   referencedDocumentRole

Definition

`referencedDocumentRole` is a classification that identifies the function of the established relationship.

Valid values
- REF (SX001G:generalDocumentReference)
- REQ (SX001G:requirementsDocumentReference)
- DRW (SX001G:drawingDocumentReference)
- VER (SX001G:verificationDocumentReference)
- VAL (SX001G:validationDocumentReference)
- DIR (SX001G:directiveDocumentReference)
- SRC (SX001G:sourceDocumentReference)
- RES (SX001G:resultDocumentReference)
- DES (SX001G:designDocumentReference)

Examples
– Document reference
– Drawing reference
– Verification
– Directive
– Source
– Design document reference

Type
– CDM ClassificationType

8 referenceDesignator

Definition

referenceDesignator is an identifier that establishes a unique designator for a location within the overall Product, and to differentiate it from other locations.

Note

Reference designators serve as a cross reference between parts contained in wiring diagrams, hydraulic systems etc. and eg, the Illustrated Parts Data (IPD).

References
– Product, refer to Chap 2.16
– identifier, refer to Chap 2.9

Valid values
– RFD (SX001G:referenceDesignator)

Type
– CDM IdentifierType

9 Remark

Definition

Remark is an <<attributeGroup>> that provides additional information about the associated item.

Note

A remark may be a personal opinion ("I prefer more onions in my soup") or it may be a technical fact ("The manufacturer recommends heating the soup to 45 degrees Celsius").

Type
– UML class

10 Remark UoF

Definition

The Remark UoF provides the capability to annotate additional information relevant to the associated item which is not part of the immediate subject.

Reference
– Remark, refer to Para 9

11 RemarkItem

Definition

RemarkItem is an <<extend>> interface that provides its associated data model to those classes that implement it.

Type
- UML <<extend>> stereotype

12 remarkText

Definition
remarkText is a description that provides the text of the additional information.

Type
- CDM DescriptorType

13 remarkType

Definition
remarkType is a classification that defines the purpose of the remark.

Valid values
- INT (SX001G:internalRemark)
- PUB (SX001G:publicRemark)
- RSP (SX001G:responseToRemark)

Examples
- Internal note
- Technical fact

Type
- CDM ClassificationType

14 removedDateTime

Definition
removedDateTime is a date and time that specifies the exact point in time when the RealizedPart was uninstalled from the InstallationLocation.

References
- InstallationLocation, refer to Chap 2.9
- RealizedPart, refer to Para 1

Type
- CDM DateTimeType

15 RepeatDefinition

Definition
RepeatDefinition is a <<class>> that represents the set of circumstances which define the PeriodicTimeLimit.

Note 1
Only one RepeatDefinition must be active at a specific moment in time.

Note 2
A threshold is a point that must not be exceeded by the TimeLimitItem once the RepeatDefinition has been activated.

Note 3
A trigger is something that activates a RepeatDefinition.

Reference
- `PeriodicTimeLimit`, refer to Chap 2.16

Type
- UML class

16 Resource Specification UoF

Definition

The Resource Specification UoF provides the capability to define generic definitions of resources needed without having to define its actual realization.

17 ResourceRealization

Definition

`ResourceRealization` is a <<relationship>> where a `ResourceSpecification` relates to an instance of `PartAsDesigned` that fulfills the resource specification.

References
- `PartAsDesigned`, refer to Chap 2.16
- `ResourceSpecification`, refer to Para 18

Type
- UML class

18 ResourceSpecification

Definition

`ResourceSpecification` is a <<class>> that defines a resource by its characteristics.

Note

`ResourceSpecification` allows for more generic resource definitions ie, a task/subtask does not need to be changed due to eg, customer specific resource preferences.

Type
- UML class

19 resourceSpecificationDescription

Definition

`resourceSpecificationDescription` is a description that gives more information on the characteristics that a part realization must fulfill in order to qualify as a possible resource.

Type
- CDM `DescriptorType`

20 resourceSpecificationIdentifier

Definition

`resourceSpecificationIdentifier` is an identifier that establishes a unique designator for a `ResourceSpecification` and to differentiate it from other instances of `ResourceSpecification`.

References
- `ResourceSpecification`, refer to Para 18
- `identifier`, refer to Chap 2.9

Valid values
- ID (SX001G:resourceSpecificationIdentifier)
- STD (SX001G:standardsReferenceDesignator)

Type
- CDM `IdentifierType`

21 resourceSpecificationName

Definition
`resourceSpecificationName` is a name by which the `ResourceSpecification` is known and can be easily referenced.

Reference
- `ResourceSpecification`, refer to Para 18

Type
- CDM `NameType`

22 ResourceSpecificationRevision

Definition
`ResourceSpecificationRevision` is a <<class>> representing an iteration applied to a `ResourceSpecification`.

Reference
- `ResourceSpecification`, refer to Para 18

Type
- UML class

23 resourceSpecificationRevisionDate

Definition
`resourceSpecificationRevisionDate` a date that specifies when the `ResourceSpecification` was revised.

Reference
- `ResourceSpecification`, refer to Para 18

Type
- CDM `DateType`

24 resourceSpecificationRevisionIdentifier

Definition
`resourceSpecificationRevisionIdentifier` is an identifier that establishes a unique designator for a `ResourceSpecificationRevision` and to differentiate it from other instances of `ResourceSpecificationRevision`.

References
- `ResourceSpecificationRevision`, refer to Para 22
- `identifier`, refer to Chap 2.9

Valid values
- ID (SX001G:resourceSpecificationRevisionIdentifier)

Type
- CDM `IdentifierType`

25   resourceSpecificationRevisionRationale

Definition

`resourceSpecificationRevisionRationale` is a description that gives more information on the justification for revising the `ResourceSpecification`.

Reference
- `ResourceSpecification`, refer to Para 18

Type
- CDM `DescriptorType`

26   resourceSpecificationRevisionStatus

Definition

`resourceSpecificationRevisionStatus` is a state that identifies the maturity of a `ResourceSpecificationRevision`.

References
- `ResourceSpecificationRevision`, refer to Para 22
- state, refer to Chap 2.19

Type
- CDM `StateType`

27   resourceSpecificationType

Definition

`resourceSpecificationType` is a classification that identifies further specialization for a `ResourceSpecification`.

Reference
- `ResourceSpecification`, refer to Para 18

Valid values
- S (SX001G:sparePart)
- R (SX001G:repairableSparePart)
- E (SX001G:expendableSparePart)
- SE (SX001G:supportEquipment)
- SSE (SX001G:safetyRelatedSupportEquipment)
- HT (SX001G:standardHandTool)
- C (SX001G:consumablePart)
- M (SX001G:rawMaterial)
- PE (SX001G:personalProtectionPart)
- EP (SX001G:expendablePersonalProtectionPart)
- PR (SX001G:productProtectionPart)
- PA (SX001G:packagingPart)
- IT (SX001G:informationTechnologyPart)
- INF (SX001G:infrastructureResource)
- CNWK (SX001G:communicationNetworkInfrastructureResource)
- TNWK (SX001G:transportNetworkInfrastructureResource)
- POW (SX001G:powerInfrastructureResource)

- HNG (SX001G:hangarInfrastructureResource)
- DOCK (SX001G:dockInfrastructureResource)
- DRYD (SX001G:dryDockInfrastructureResource)
- COMP (SX001G:computerInfrastructureResource)
- GAR (SX001G:garageInfrastructureResource)

Type
- CDM `ClassificationType`

28   ResultingDataModule

Definition

`ResultingDataModule` is a <<relationship>> that identifies a data module issue in which a `TaskRevision` is further detailed.

Note

A data module can contain either a complete or partial description of a given task revision.

Reference
- `TaskRevision`, refer to Chap 2.20

Type
- UML class

Page intentionally blank.

Chapter 2.19

Glossary - S

Table of contents

List of tables

References

Table 1 References

Chap No./Document No.	Title
Chap 2.1	Glossary - A
Chap 2.2	Glossary - B
Chap 2.4	Glossary - D
Chap 2.5	Glossary - E
Chap 2.9	Glossary - I
Chap 2.13	Glossary - M
Chap 2.14	Glossary - N
Chap 2.15	Glossary - O
Chap 2.16	Glossary - P
Chap 2.20	Glossary - T
Chap 2.21	Glossary - U
Chap 2.22	Glossary - V
Chap 2.23	Glossary - W

1   S1000DDataModule

Definition

S1000DDataModule is a Document that is written in accordance with an S1000D schema.

Reference

- Document, refer to Chap 2.4

Type

- UML class

2   S1000DDataModuleIssue

Definition

S1000DDataModuleIssue is a DocumentIssue that identifies a specific issue of a data module produced in accordance with S1000D.

Reference

- DocumentIssue, refer to Chap 2.4

Type

- UML class

3   S1000DPublicationModule

Definition

`S1000DPublicationModule` is a `Document` that identifies a publication published in accordance with S1000D.

Reference

- `Document`, refer to Chap 2.4

Type

- UML class

4   S1000DPublicationModuleIssue

Definition

`S1000DPublicationModuleIssue` is a `DocumentIssue` that identifies a specific issue of a publication module published in accordance with S1000D.

Reference

- `DocumentIssue`, refer to Chap 2.4

Type

- UML class

5   SamplingDefinition

Definition

`SamplingDefinition` is an <<attributeGroup>> that specifies whether the associated action is to be performed on a subset of the population of the associated target item.

Type

- UML class

6   SamplingItem

Definition

`SamplingItem` is an <<extend>> interface that represents the common behavior for those classes which can have an associated `SamplingDefinition`.

Reference

- `SamplingDefinition`, refer to Para 5

Type

- UML <<extend>> stereotype

7   samplingMethodDescription

Definition

`samplingMethodDescription` is a description that gives more information on the way in which the sample must be selected.

Type

- CDM `DescriptorType`

8 samplingValue

Definition

samplingValue is a property that specifies the number or fraction of the total population to be selected.

Type
- CDM PropertyType

9 second

Definition

second is an Integer that represents the second within a minute expressed as a value between '0' and '59'.

References
- minute, refer to Chap 2.13
- value, refer to Chap 2.22

Type
- UML integer

10 Security Classification UoF

Definition

The Security Classification UoF provides the capability to assign security classifications to objects that need special handling for protection against unauthorized access or distribution.

11 SecurityClass

Definition

SecurityClass is a <<class>> that identifies a level of confidentiality which can be used to protect something against unauthorized access.

Type
- UML class

12 SecurityClassification

Definition

SecurityClassification is a <<relationship>> that associates a given SecurityClass with the item that must be protected against unauthorized access or distribution

Reference
- SecurityClass, refer to Para 11

Type
- UML class

13 securityClassificationAuthority

Definition

securityClassificationAuthority identifies the Organization that is the authoritative source for the defined SecurityClassification.

References
- Organization, refer to Chap 2.15

- SecurityClassification, refer to Para 12

Type
- CDM Organization

14 securityClassificationDate

Definition
securityClassificationDate is a date when the security classification is declared.

Type
- CDM DateType

15 SecurityClassificationItem

Definition
SecurityClassificationItem is an <<extend>> interface that provides its associated data model to those classes that implement it.

Type
- UML <<extend>> stereotype

16 securityClassValue

Definition
securityClassValue is a name that defines the level of confidentiality.

Examples
- Unclassified
- Restricted
- Top secret
- Secret
- Confidential
- Company confidential

Type
- CDM NameType

17 sense

Definition
sense is a word or a code that defines the direction of the offset.

Type
- CDM validValue

18 Serialized Part Configuration UoF

Definition
The Serialized Part Configuration UoF provides the capability to identify parts contained within a serialized part.

19 Serialized Product Variant Configuration UoF

Definition
The Serialized Product Variant Configuration UoF provides the capability to identify combinations of actual installation locations for a given serialized product variant and actual parts that are or have been installed at the respective installation location.

Reference
- `Product`, refer to Chap 2.16

20 SerializedAssertItem

Definition

`SerializedAssertItem` is a <<select>> interface that identifies classes from which an instance can be used as the `EvaluationByAssertionOfSerializedItems` assert item.

Reference
- `EvaluationByAssertionOfSerializedItems`, refer to Chap 2.5

Type
- UML <<select>> stereotype

21 SerializedHardwarePart

Definition

`SerializedHardwarePart` is <<class>> that represent an actual physical part which can be identified as an individual.

Note 1

A `SerializedHardwarePart` is usually referred to as "Equipment". This name has not been used in the data model so as to distinguish between the generic equipment and the individual ones.

Note 2

A `SerializedHardwarePart` may evolve due to modifications. The actual build standard at a given moment is defined through the relationship `SerializedPartDesignAssociation`.

Type
- UML class

22 SerializedHardwarePartModification

Definition

`SerializedHardwarePartModification` is a <<relationship>> where a modified `SerializedHardwarePart` relates back to its previous design standard and its history.

Reference
- `SerializedHardwarePart`, refer to Para 21

Type
- UML class

23 serializedHardwarePartModificationDate

Definition

`serializedHardwarePartModificationDate` is a date that identifies when a `SerializedHardwarePart` changed its design standard.

Reference
- `SerializedHardwarePart`, refer to Para 21

Type
- CDM DateType

24   serializedPartIdentifier

Definition

serializedPartIdentifier is an identifier that establishes a unique designator for a SerializedHardwarePart and to differentiate it from other instances of SerializedHardwarePart.

Note

SerializedHardwarePart must be unique in the context of its partDefinitionIdentifier.

References
- SerializedHardwarePart, refer to Para 21
- identifier, refer to Chap 2.9

Valid values
- ID (SX001G:serializedPartIdentifier)

Type
- CDM IdentifierType

25   SerializedPartsListPosition

Definition

SerializedPartsListPosition is a <<class>> that represents a position within the associated SerializedHardwarePart.

Reference
- SerializedHardwarePart, refer to Para 21

Type
- UML class

26   serializedPartsListPositionIdentifier

Definition

serializedPartsListPositionIdentifier is an identifier that establishes a unique designator for a SerializedPartsListPosition and to differentiate it from other instances of SerializedPartsListPosition.

References
- SerializedPartsListPosition, refer to Para 25
- identifier, refer to Chap 2.9

Valid values
- ID (SX001G:serializedPartsListPositionIdentifier)

Type
- CDM IdentifierType

27   serializedPartsListPositionName

Definition

serializedPartsListPositionName is a name by which the
SerializedPartsListPosition is known and can be easily referenced.

Reference

- SerializedPartsListPosition, refer to Para 25

Type

- CDM NameType

28   SerializedProductVariant

Definition

SerializedProductVariant is <<class>> that represent an actual product variant
which is identified as an individual.

Note

A SerializedProductVariant must be manufactured in accordance with its
definition as defined by its productVariantIdentifier.

Type

- UML class

29   SerializedProductVariantConfigurationConformance

Definition

SerializedProductVariantConfigurationConformance is a
<<relationship>> that identifies the allowed product configuration to which the
SerializedProductVariant complies with during a defined period of time.

Reference

- SerializedProductVariant, refer to Para 28

Type

- UML class

30   serializedProductVariantIdentifier

Definition

serializedProductVariantIdentifier is an identifier that establishes a unique
designator for a SerializedProductVariant and to differentiate it from other
instances of SerializedProductVariant.

References

- SerializedProductVariant, refer to Para 28
- identifier, refer to Chap 2.9

Valid values

- ID (SX001G:serializedProductVariantIdentifier)

Type

- CDM IdentifierType

31 SerialNumberRange

Definition

SerialNumberRange is a <<compoundAttribute>> that identifies an interval of serialized items.

Note

The range pattern may be open-ended.

Type

– UML class

32 Service

Definition

Service is an activity where technical, physical or intellectual work is performed for another party to fulfill a need or demand.

Note

Does not cover activities that deliver a physical product.

Reference

– Party, refer to Chap 2.16

Examples

– Equipment repair
– Availability study
– Car wash
– Facility (re)painting

Type

– Business Term

33 SingleValuePropertyType

Definition

SingleValuePropertyType is a NumericalPropertyType that specifies a single value and its unit.

References

– NumericalPropertyType, refer to Chap 2.14
– unit, refer to Chap 2.21
– value, refer to Chap 2.22

Type

– UML class

34 Skill

Definition

Skill is a term that represents human cognitive, psychomotor, and affective abilities.

Reference

– Term, refer to Chap 2.20

Type

– Business Term

35 Skill

Definition

Skill is a <<class>> that represents human cognitive, psychomotor, and affective abilities.

Type
- UML class

36 skillCode

Definition

skillCode is an identifier that establishes a unique designator for a Skill and to differentiate it from other instances of Skill.

References
- Skill, refer to Para 34
- identifier, refer to Chap 2.9

Valid values
- ID (SX001G:skillCode)

Type
- CDM IdentifierType

37 Skill level

Definition

Skill level is a term that represents a defined proficiency of a trade.

References
- Trade, refer to Chap 2.20
- Term, refer to Chap 2.20

Type
- Business Term

38 SkillLevel

Definition

SkillLevel is a <<class>> that represents a defined proficiency of a Trade.

Reference
- Trade, refer to Chap 2.20

Type
- UML class

39 skillLevelDescription

Definition

skillLevelDescription is a description that gives more information on a proficiency.

Type
- CDM DescriptorType

40   skillLevelName

Definition

`skillLevelName` is a name that uniquely establishes a proficiency.

Type
- CDM `NameType`

41   Software Element UoF

Definition

The Software Element UoF provides the capability to specify that an element within a breakdown is software and can be associated with the software part(s) that fulfill the requirement.

42   SoftwareElement

Definition

`SoftwareElement` is a `BreakdownElement` that is realized as a `SoftwarePartAsDesigned`.

References
- `BreakdownElement`, refer to Chap 2.2
- `SoftwarePartAsDesigned`, refer to Para 48

Type
- UML class

43   softwareElementModificationFrequency

Definition

`softwareElementModificationFrequency` is a property that defines the expected frequency with which the `SoftwarePartAsDesigned` which realizes this `SoftwareElementRevision` will be modified.

References
- `SoftwareElementRevision`, refer to Para 45
- `SoftwarePartAsDesigned`, refer to Para 48

Examples
- 5 years
- 3 months

Type
- CDM `PropertyType`

44   SoftwareElementPartRealization

Definition

`SoftwareElementPartRealization` is a <<relationship>> where a `SoftwareElementRevision` relates to an instance of `SoftwarePartAsDesigned` which fulfills the `SoftwareElement` specification.

References
- `SoftwareElement`, refer to Para 42
- `SoftwareElementRevision`, refer to Para 45

- SoftwarePartAsDesigned, refer to Para 48

Type
- UML class

45   SoftwareElementRevision

Definition

SoftwareElementRevision is a BreakdownElementRevision representing an iteration applied to a SoftwareElement.

References
- BreakdownElementRevision, refer to Chap 2.2
- SoftwareElement, refer to Para 42

Type
- UML class

46   softwareElementSize

Definition

softwareElementSize is a property that defines the size of the SoftwarePartAsDesigned which realizes this SoftwareElementRevision.

References
- SoftwareElementRevision, refer to Para 45
- SoftwarePartAsDesigned, refer to Para 48

Examples
- 800 Kbytes - contracted
- 23.5 Mbytes - executable
- 10.000 lines of code - estimated

Type
- CDM PropertyType

47   softwareElementType

Definition

softwareElementType is a classification that identifies further specialization for a SoftwareElement.

Reference
- SoftwareElement, refer to Para 42

Valid values
- L (SX001G:loadableSofwareElement)
- D (SX001G:distributedSoftwareElement)
- E (SX001G:embeddedSofwareElement)

Type
- CDM ClassificationType

48   SoftwarePartAsDesigned

Definition

`SoftwarePartAsDesigned` is a `PartAsDesigned` that is produced as an
executable software or as a data file.

Note

Non-executable software includes eg, maps.

Reference

- `PartAsDesigned`, refer to Chap 2.16

Type

- UML class

49   SoftwarePartAsReleased

Definition

`SoftwarePartAsReleased` is <<class>> that represents actual build of a software
which is delivered.

Type

- UML class

50   softwareReleaseIdentifier

Definition

`softwareReleaseIdentifier` is an identifier that establishes a unique designator for
a software build and to differentiate it from other instances of software build.

Reference

- `identifier`, refer to Chap 2.9

Valid values

- ID (SX001G:softwareReleaseIdentifier)

Type

- CDM `IdentifierType`

51   sourceDocumentPortion

Definition

`sourceDocumentPortion` is a description that gives more information on relevant
portions of the related document.

Type

- CDM `DescriptorType`

52   Special Event UoF

Definition

The Special Event UoF provides the capability to define typical happenings which can be
induced to an item under analysis and which can impact the operational capability of the
`Product` during its in-service phase.

Reference

- `Product`, refer to Chap 2.16

53 SpecialEventAnalysis

Definition

`SpecialEventAnalysis` is an `AnalysisActivity` that represents the objective for, and outcome of, a special event analysis carried out for the AnalysisCandidateItem.

References
- `AnalysisActivity`, refer to Chap 2.1
- `AnalysisCandidateItem`, refer to Chap 2.1

Type
- UML class

54 SpecialEventAnalysisRevision

Definition

`SpecialEventAnalysisRevision` is an `AnalysisActivityRevision` representing an iteration applied to a `SpecialEventAnalysis`.

Reference
- `SpecialEventAnalysis`, refer to Para 53

Type
- UML class

55 SpecialEventDefinition

Definition

`SpecialEventDefinition` is a <<class>>that represents a typical happening which can be induced to the item under analysis during its normal operation, and can lead to damages.

Type
- UML class

56 specialEventDefinitionCauseCategory

Definition

`specialEventDefinitionCauseCategory` is a classification that identifies a generalization that organize special events into an overarching special event taxonomy.

Valid values
- EXT (SX001G:externalCauseSpecialEvent)
- NAT (SX001G:naturalPhenomenonSpecialEvent)
- MET (SX001G:meteorologicalSpecialEvent)
- ANI (SX001G:animalSpecialEvent)
- HUM (SX001G:humanImpactSpecialEvent)
- CBT (SX001G:combatSpecialEvent)
- MAN (SX001G:materialManeuverSpecialEvent)
- INT (SX001G:internalSpecialEvent)
- DYS (SX001G:internalDysfunctionSpecialEvent)
- HEA (SX001G:extensiveHeatSpecialEvent)
- VIB (SX001G:extensiveVibrationSpecialEvent)

Type
- CDM `ClassificationType`

57   specialEventDefinitionDecription

Definition

`specialEventDefinitionDecription` is a description that gives more information on the `SpecialEventDefinition`.

Reference

- `SpecialEventDefinition`, refer to <u>Para 55</u>

Type

- CDM `DescriptorType`

58   specialEventDefinitionName

Definition

`specialEventDefinitionName` is a name by which the `SpecialEventDefinition` is known and can be easily referenced.

Reference

- `SpecialEventDefinition`, refer to <u>Para 55</u>

Type

- CDM `NameType`

59   specialEventDefinitionOccurrenceValue

Definition

`specialEventDefinitionOccurrenceValue` is a property that quantifies how often a defined special event is likely to occur.

Type

- CDM `PropertyType`

60   specialEventOccurenceRatio

Definition

`specialEventOccurenceRatio` identifies the fraction of an individual `SpecialEventDefinition` in relation to the entire population of special events identified for the Product that will occur in relation to the associated `ProductUsagePhase`.

References

- `Product`, refer to <u>Chap 2.16</u>
- `ProductUsagePhase`, refer to <u>Chap 2.16</u>
- `SpecialEventDefinition`, refer to <u>Para 55</u>

Type

- CDM `PropertyType`

61   SpecialEventProductUsagePhaseOccurrence

Definition

`SpecialEventProductUsagePhaseOccurrence` is a <<relationship>> that defines an association between an instance of `SpecialEventDefinition` and an instance of `ProductUsagePhase` during which the special event can occur.

References
-   ProductUsagePhase, refer to Chap 2.16
-   SpecialEventDefinition, refer to Para 55

Type
-   UML class

62 Sphere

Definition
Sphere represents a three-dimensional object where every point on its surface is equidistant from its center.

Type
-   UML class

63 state

Definition
state is a word or a code that defines the particular condition that something is in.

Type
-   CDM validValue

64 stateRecordingDateTime

Definition
stateRecordingDateTime is a calendar date and time that identifies when the state was established.

Reference
-   state, refer to Para 63

Type
-   CDM DateTimeType

65 StateType

Definition
StateType is an S-Series IPS specifications defined <<primitive>> that represents a particular condition that something is in at a particular time.

Type
-   UML class

66 StreetAddress

Definition
StreetAddress is a <<class> that represents a locatable position along a road.

Type
-   UML class

67 streetName

Definition
streetName is the name by which a road is officially known and can be easily referenced.

Examples
- E-2561 Road
- Main Street

Type
- CDM NameType

68 streetNumber

Definition
streetNumber is a string of characters that represents the position along a street

Examples
- 4
- 35.5 km

Type
- UML string

69 SubstanceDefinition

Definition
SubstanceDefinition is a <<class>> that identifies high concern physical matter.

Examples
- REACH (Registration, Evaluation, Authorisation and Restriction of Chemicals)
- CAS (Chemical Abstract Substance) Registry

Type
- UML class

70 substanceIdentifier

Definition
substanceIdentifier is an identifier that establishes a unique designator for a
SubstanceDefinition and to differentiate it from other instances of
SubstanceDefinition.

References
- SubstanceDefinition, refer to Para 69
- identifier, refer to Chap 2.9

Valid values
- ID (SX001G:substanceIdentifier)
- CAS (SX001G:chemicalAbstractsServiceRegistryNumber)

Type
- CDM IdentifierType

71 substanceName

Definition
substanceName is a name by which the SubstanceDefinition is known and can
be easily referenced.

Reference
- SubstanceDefinition, refer to Para 69

Type
- CDM `NameType`

72   SubstitutePartAsDesigned

Definition
`SubstitutePartAsDesigned` is a <<relationship>> that defines a substitute
`PartAsDesignedPartsListEntry` which can replace the base
`PartAsDesignedPartsListEntry` in the context of the parent
`PartAsDesignedPartsList`.

References
- `PartAsDesignedPartsList`, refer to Chap 2.16
- `PartAsDesignedPartsListEntry`, refer to Chap 2.16

Type
- UML class

73   subSubSystem

Definition
`subSubSystem` is a string of characters that represents the sub-subsystem attribute of the
data module code.

Note
   A `subSubSystem` must be created in accordance with the rules defined in S1000D.

Type
- UML string

74   subSystem

Definition
`subSystem` is a string of characters that represents the subsystem attribute of the data
module code.

Note
   A `subSystem` must be created in accordance with the rules defined in S1000D.

Type
- UML string

75   Subtask

Definition
`Subtask` is a <<class>> that represents the specification of a work step that is to be
performed as part of a `Task`.

Reference
- `Task`, refer to Chap 2.20

Type
- UML class

76   SubtaskByDefinition

Definition

SubtaskByDefinition is a Subtask that provides detailed information of the defined work step.

Reference

–   Subtask, refer to Para 75

Type

–   UML class

77   SubtaskByTaskReference

Definition

SubtaskByTaskReference is a Subtask where the details of the subtask are defined as a separate Task.

References

–   Subtask, refer to Para 75
–   Task, refer to Chap 2.20

Type

–   UML class

78   subtaskDescription

Definition

subtaskDescription is a description of the procedure performed during the Subtask.

Reference

–   Subtask, refer to Para 75

Type

–   CDM DescriptorType

79   subtaskDuration

Definition

subtaskDuration is a property that specifies the average time required for the performance of a Subtask, regardless of the number of personnel working simultaneously.

Note

subtaskDuration does not include time spent awaiting spares, support equipment, facilities or personnel (logistics delay time).

Reference

–   Subtask, refer to Para 75

Type

–   CDM PropertyType

80   subtaskEndItemObjectiveState

Definition

subtaskEndItemObjectiveState is a state that identifies the condition of the product that will exist after the accomplishment of the Subtask.

References
- Subtask, refer to <u>Para 75</u>
- state, refer to <u>Para 63</u>

Valid values
- EL (SX001G:elecricalPowerEstablishedEndItemState)
- WS (SX001G:waterSupplyEstablishedEndItemState)
- HP (SX001G:hydraulicPowerEstablishedEndItemState)
- TC (SX001G:taskCheckedEndItemState)
- DF (SX001G:defueledEndItemState)
- CS (SX001G:controlStatusEstablishedEndItemState)
- AS (SX001G:airSupplyEstablishedEndItemState)
- ELX (SX001G:externalElecricalPowerEstablishedEndItemState)
- ELI (SX001G:internalElecricalPowerEstablishedEndItemState)
- ELE (SX001G:elecricalPowerFromEngineEstablishedEndItemState)
- FU (SX001G:fueledEndItemState)
- ELA (SX001G:elecricalPowerFromAPUEstablishedEndItemState)
- JC (SX001G:jackedEndItemState)
- UJ (SX001G:unjackedEndItemState)
- SY (SX001G:safetyDeviceEstablishedEndItemState)

Type
- CDM StateType

81 subtaskIdentifier

Definition
subtaskIdentifier is an identifier that establishes a unique designator for a Subtask and to differentiate it from other instances of Subtask.

Note
A Subtask is identified within the context of a specific Task.

References
- Subtask, refer to <u>Para 75</u>
- identifier, refer to <u>Chap 2.9</u>

Valid values
- ID (SX001G:subtaskIdentifier)

Type
- CDM IdentifierType

82 subtaskInformationCode

Definition
subtaskInformationCode is a classification that identifies the main purpose for the Subtask.

Note
An informationCode must be created in accordance with the rules defined in S1000D.

Reference
- Subtask, refer to <u>Para 75</u>

Type
- CDM `ClassificationType`

83   SubtaskInZone

Definition
`SubtaskInZone` is a <<relationship>> that identifies the zone where the `Subtask` is to be performed.

Reference
- `Subtask`, refer to <u>Para 75</u>

Type
- UML class

84   subtaskMaintenanceLocation

Definition
`subtaskMaintenanceLocation` is a classification that specifies where the Subtask will be performed in relation to the product.

Note
Proposed values equal the S1000D Item Location Codes.

Reference
- `Subtask`, refer to <u>Para 75</u>

Valid values
- B (SX001G:maintenanceOnItemOnMajorAssembly)
- A (SX001G:maintenanceOnItemWhenInstalledOnProduct)
- C (SX001G:imaintenanceOnBench)
- D (SX001G:maintenanceAnywhere)

Type
- CDM `ClassificationType`

85   subtaskName

Definition
`subtaskName` is a name by which the Subtask is known and can be easily referenced.

Reference
- `Subtask`, refer to <u>Para 75</u>

Type
- CDM `NameType`

86   subtaskRole

Definition
`subtaskRole` is a classification that identifies how the Subtask is related to the main function of the `Task`.

Note
`SubtaskRole` enables mapping between S3000L and the main portions of the S1000D procedure schema.

References
- Subtask, refer to Para 75
- Task, refer to Chap 2.20

Valid values
- ST (SX001G:startupSubtask)
- CL (SX001G:closeupSubtask)
- COR (SX001G:coreSubtask)
- CON (SX001G:coreNoRequiredConditionsSubtask)

Type
- CDM ClassificationType

87 SubtaskSourceDocument

Definition

SubtaskSourceDocument is a <<relationship>> that identifies an external Document where the Subtask is originally defined and more details are given.

References
- Document, refer to Chap 2.4
- Subtask, refer to Para 75

Type
- UML class

88 SubtaskTarget

Definition

SubtaskTarget is a <<relationship>> that identifies the item on which the Subtask is to be performed.

Reference
- Subtask, refer to Para 75

Type
- UML class

89 SubtaskTargetItem

Definition

SubtaskTargetItem is a <<select>> interface that identifies items on which a Subtask can be performed.

Reference
- Subtask, refer to Para 75

Type
- UML <<select>> stereotype

90 SubtaskTimeline

Definition

SubtaskTimeline is a <<relationship>> that identifies that there is a time dependency between two Subtasks within the same Task.

Reference
- Task, refer to Chap 2.20

Type
- UML class

91 subtaskTimelineEvent

Definition
subtaskTimelineEvent is a classification that identifies how the starting point for a Subtask depends upon its preceding Subtask

Reference
- Subtask, refer to Para 75

Valid values
- END (SX001G:subtaskEndEvent)
- START (SX001G:subtaskStartEvent)

Type
- CDM ClassificationType

92 subtaskTimelineLag

Definition
subtaskTimelineLag is a property that specifies the time that must elapse before the Subtask under consideration can start, in relation to its associated timeline event.

Reference
- Subtask, refer to Para 75

Type
- CDM PropertyType

93 SubtaskWarningCautionNote

Definition
SubtaskWarningCautionNote is a <<relationship>> that identifies a WarningCautionNote that is associated with a given Subtask.

References
- Subtask, refer to Para 75
- WarningCautionNote, refer to Chap 2.23

Type
- UML class

94 Supplier

Definition
Supplier is a party that provides a particular service or product.

Note
Use the term supplier not vendor

References
- Party, refer to Chap 2.16
- Product, refer to Chap 2.16

- Service, refer to <u>Para 32</u>

Type
- Business Term

95 Support concept

Definition

Support concept is a description that provides general considerations, constraints, and plans for interim and long-term sustainment of the item under analysis.

Note

Support concept can include support locations, responsibilities, period of time etc.

Reference
- Item, refer to <u>Chap 2.9</u>

Type
- Business Term

96 SupportingTask

Definition

SupportingTask is a Task that does not meet a TaskRequirement, but identifies a set of work steps which will be carried out as part of multiple Tasks.

Note 1

The objective for a SupportingTask is to enable reuse of a sequence of work steps, needed by a set of Tasks.

Note 2

A SupportingTask will only be used in the context of SubtaskByTaskReference.

References
- Task, refer to <u>Chap 2.20</u>
- TaskRequirement, refer to <u>Chap 2.20</u>

Examples
- Jack vehicle
- Open hatch

Type
- UML class

97 SupportingTaskUsage

Definition

SupportingTaskUsage is a TaskUsage that expands the definition of an embedded reusable Task in the context of a given support solution.

Note

A SupportingTask has no special characterizations apart from a TaskFrequency since it will never be performed on its own.

References
- Task, refer to <u>Chap 2.20</u>
- TaskUsage, refer to <u>Chap 2.20</u>

Type
- UML class

98   system

Definition

system is a string of characters that represents the system attribute of the data module code.

Note

A system must be created in accordance with the rules defined in S1000D.

Type
- UML string

99   systemDifferenceCode

Definition

systemDifferenceCode is a string of characters that represents the system difference code attribute of the data module code.

Note

A systemDifferenceCode must be created in accordance with the rules defined in S1000D.

Reference
- system, refer to Para 98

Type
- UML string

Page intentionally blank.

Chapter 2.20

Glossary - T

Table of contents

List of tables

References

Table 1 References

Chap No./Document No.	Title
Chap 2.4	Glossary - D
Chap 2.5	Glossary - E
Chap 2.9	Glossary - I
Chap 2.16	Glossary - P
Chap 2.19	Glossary - S
Chap 2.22	Glossary - V
Chap 2.23	Glossary - W

1 Task requirement

Definition

Task requirement is a term that identifies the need for a task to be developed and documented.

Note

A task requirement can be operational, preventive, corrective etc.

Reference

– Task, refer to Para 4

Example

– A preventive maintenance task requirement identifies the need to develop a task that specifies how to replace the oil filter on an engine after 1000 operating hours.

Type

– Business Term

2 Task Requirement UoF

Definition

The Task Requirement UoF supports early documentation of the need for a task to be performed to support a Product.

References

– Product, refer to Chap 2.16
– Task, refer to Para 5

3 Task Resource UoF

Definition

The Task Resource UoF supports a detailed specification of resources needed to perform a specified amount of work.

Reference

– Task, refer to Para 5

4 Task

Definition

Task is an item that represents the specification of work to be done or undertaken with a defined beginning and end.

Reference

- Item, refer to Chap 2.9

Type

- Business Term

5 Task

Definition

Task is a <<class>> that represents the specification of work to be done or undertaken.

Type

- UML class

6 Task UoF

Definition

The Task UoF supports the detailed definition of tasks required to support a Product.

References

- Product, refer to Chap 2.16
- Task, refer to Para 5

7 Task Usage UoF

Definition

The Task Usage UoF provides the capability to expand the definition for the execution of a task in the context of a given support solution.

Reference

- Task, refer to Para 5

8 TaskAnalysisItem

Definition

TaskAnalysisItem is an <<extend>> interface that provides its associated data model to those classes that implement it.

Type

- UML <<extend>> stereotype

9 TaskDocumentResource

Definition

TaskDocumentResource is a TaskResource that identifies a Document used as a resource.

References

- Document, refer to Chap 2.4
- TaskResource, refer to Para 47

Example

– A form that must be filled out before, during or after the specified amount of work is carried out.

Type

– UML class

10 taskDuration

Definition

`taskDuration` is a property that specifies the average time required for the performance of a `Task`, regardless of the number of personnel working simultaneously .

Note 1

`taskDuration` could be calculated from the subtask durations.

Note 2

`taskDuration` does not include time spent awaiting spares, support equipment, facilities or personnel (logistics delay time).

Reference

– `Task`, refer to Para 5

Type

– CDM `PropertyType`

11 TaskFrequency

Definition

`TaskFrequency` is an <<attributeGroup>> that specifies the rate of occurrence of a Task in its defined usage.

Reference

– `Task`, refer to Para 5

Type

– UML class

12 taskFrequencyCalculationMethod

Definition

`taskFrequencyCalculationMethod` is a description that provides further information on how the `TaskFrequencyValue` has been derived.

Type

– CDM `DescriptorType`

13 taskFrequencyValue

Definition

`taskFrequencyValue` is a property that represents the rate of occurrence value.

Reference

– `value`, refer to Chap 2.22

Type

– CDM `PropertyType`

14   taskIdentifier

Definition

`taskIdentifier` is an identifier that establishes a unique designator for a `Task` and to differentiate it from other instances of Task.

References
- `Task`, refer to Para 5
- `identifier`, refer to Chap 2.9

Valid values
- ID (SX001G:taskIdentifier)

Type
- CDM `IdentifierType`

15   taskInformationCode

Definition

`taskInformationCode` is a classification that identifies the main purpose for the Task.

Note

Valid classifications are defined in the ASD IPS Specification S1000D, Technical Publications using a Common Source Database.

Reference
- `Task`, refer to Para 5

Type
- CDM ClassificationType

16   TaskInfrastructureResource

Definition

`TaskInfrastructureResource` is a `TaskResource` that defines foundational systems and services required as a resource.

Reference
- `TaskResource`, refer to Para 47

Type
UML class

17   taskInfrastructureResourceCategory

Definition

`taskInfrastructureResourceCategory` is a classification that identifies further specialization for a `TaskInfrastructureResource`.

Reference
- `TaskInfrastructureResource`, refer to Para 16

Valid values
- CNWK (SX001G:communicationNetworkInfrastructureResource)
- TNWK (SX001G:transportNetworkInfrastructureResource)
- POW (SX001G:powerInfrastructureResource)
- HNG (SX001G:hangarInfrastructureResource)
- DOCK (SX001G:dockInfrastructureResource)

- DRYD (SX001G:dryDockInfrastructureResource)
- GAR (SX001G:garageInfrastructureResource)
- COMP (SX001G:computerInfrastructureResource)

Type
- CDM `ClassificationType`

18   taskInfrastructureResourceQuantity

Definition

`taskInfrastructureResourceQuantity` is a property that specifies the number of the `TaskInfrastructureResource`.

Reference
- `TaskInfrastructureResource`, refer to Para 16

Type
- CDM `PropertyType`

19   TaskJustification

Definition

`TaskJustification` is a <<relationship>> that identifies a `TaskRequirement` that defines the need for the existence of a `Task`.

References
- `Task`, refer to Para 5
- `TaskRequirement`, refer to Para 30

Type
- UML class

20   TaskLocationItem

Definition

`TaskLocationItem` is a <<select>> interface that identifies items where Tasks can be performed.

Type
- UML <<select>> stereotype

21   TaskMaterialResource

Definition

`TaskMaterialResource` is a `TaskResource` that identifies parts which are required as a resource.

Reference
- `TaskResource`, refer to Para 47

Type
- UML class

22   taskMaterialResourceCategory

Definition

`taskMaterialResourceCategory` is a classification that defines the role of the `TaskMaterialResource` in the context of the specified `Task`.

References

- `Task`, refer to Para 5
- `TaskMaterialResource`, refer to Para 21

Valid values

- S (SX001G:sparePart)
- SE (SX001G:supportEquipment)
- C (SX001G:consumablePart)
- R (SX001G:repairableSparePart)
- E (SX001G:expendableSparePart)
- SSE (SX001G:safetyRelatedSupportEquipment)
- HT (SX001G:standardHandTool)
- M (SX001G:rawMaterial)
- PE (SX001G:personalProtectionPart)
- EP (SX001G:expendablePersonalProtectionPart)
- PR (SX001G:productProtectionPart)
- PA (SX001G:packagingPart)
- IT (SX001G:informationTechnologyPart)

Type

- CDM `ClassificationType`

23   taskMaterialResourceQuantity

Definition

`taskMaterialResourceQuantity` is a property that specifies the number of a `TaskMaterialResource`.

Reference

- `TaskMaterialResource`, refer to Para 21

Type

- CDM `PropertyType`

24   taskName

Definition

`taskName` is a name by which the `Task` is known and can be easily referenced.

Reference

- `Task`, refer to Para 5

Type

- CDM `NameType`

25   TaskPersonnelResource

Definition

`TaskPersonnelResource` is a `TaskResource` that specifies the man power required as a resource.

Reference
- `TaskResource`, refer to <u>Para 47</u>

Type
- UML class

26 TaskPersonnelResourceCompetence

Definition
`TaskPersonnelResourceCompetence` is a <<relationship>> that identifies the proficiency required for `TaskPersonnelResource`.

Reference
- `TaskPersonnelResource`, refer to <u>Para 25</u>

Type
- UML class

27 taskPersonnelResourceLaborTime

Definition
`taskPersonnelResourceLaborTime` is a property that specifies the time expended by the required `TaskPersonnelResource`.

Note
Labor time can be given as single values but also as ranges or as text eg, "AsRequired".

Reference
- `TaskPersonnelResource`, refer to <u>Para 25</u>

Type
- CDM `PropertyType`

28 taskPersonnelResourceQuantity

Definition
`taskPersonnelResourceQuantity` is a property that specifies the number of the required `TaskPersonnelResource`

Note
Quantities can be given as single values but also as ranges or as text eg, "AsRequired".

Reference
- `TaskPersonnelResource`, refer to <u>Para 25</u>

Type
- CDM `PropertyType`

29 taskPersonnelResourceRole

Definition
`taskPersonnelResourceRole` is a classification that defines the purpose of the required `TaskPersonnelResource`.

Reference
- `TaskPersonnelResource`, refer to <u>Para 25</u>

Valid values
– P (SX001G:performerTaskPersonnelResource)
– Q (SX001G:qualityAssuranceTaskPersonnelResource)
– S (SX001G:supervisorTaskPersonnelResource)
– A (SX001G:assistientTaskPersonnelResource)

Examples
– Performer
– Supervisor
– Quality assurance

Type
– CDM `ClassificationType`

30   TaskRequirement

Definition

`TaskRequirement` is a <<class>> that represents the need for a procedure to be developed and documented.

Note 1

Examples of support analysis activities which result in a set of documented task requirements are: Preventive maintenance analysis (refer to S4000P) and special event analysis.

Note 2

Task requirements are identified and documented prior to any detailed task analysis.

Note 3

A task requirement can have more than one task being developed for different usage scenarios.

Type
– UML class

31   TaskRequirementAnalysisItem

Definition

`TaskRequirementAnalysisItem` is an <<extend>> interface that provides its associated data model to those classes that implement it.

Type
– UML <<extend>> stereotype

32   taskRequirementAuthority

Definition

`taskRequirementAuthority` identifies the organization that is the authoritative source for the identified `TaskRequirement`.

Reference
– `TaskRequirement`, refer to Para 30

Type
– CDM `Organization`

33   taskRequirementAuthoritySourceType

Definition

`taskRequirementAuthoritySourceType` is a classification that indicates the significance of the source from which `TaskRequirement` is derived.

Reference
- `TaskRequirement`, refer to Para 30

Valid values
- PMEC (SX001G:preventiveMaintenanceEffectCategory)
- CMR (SX001G:certificationMaintenanceRequirement)
- LEMR (SX001G:lawEnforcedMaintenanceRequirement)
- EZAP (SX001G:enhancedZonalAnalysisProgram)

Type
- CDM `ClassificationType`

34   taskRequirementDescription

Definition

`taskRequirementDescription` is a description that summarizes the procedure that needs to be performed based on the outcome of a support analysis activity.

Type
- CDM `DescriptorType`

35   taskRequirementIdentifier

Definition

`taskRequirementIdentifier` is an identifier that establishes a unique designator for a `TaskRequirement` and to differentiate it from other instances of `TaskRequirement`.

References
- `TaskRequirement`, refer to Para 30
- `identifier`, refer to Chap 2.9

Valid values
- ID (SX001G:taskRequirementIdentifier)

Type
- CDM `IdentifierType`

36   taskRequirementInformationCode

Definition

`taskRequirementInformationCode` is a classification that identifies the main purpose for the `TaskRequirement`.

Note

Valid classifications are defined in the ASD ILS Specification S1000D, Technical Publications using a Common Source Database.

Reference
- `TaskRequirement`, refer to Para 30

Type
- CDM `ClassificationType`

37   TaskRequirementJustification

Definition
`TaskRequirementJustification` is a <<relationship>> that identifies a source
which defines the need for a task.

Type
- UML class

38   taskRequirementJustificationDescription

Definition
`taskRequirementJustificationDescription` is a description that
summarizes the need for a `Task` to meet the results from a support analysis activity.

Reference
- `Task`, refer to Para 5

Type
- CDM `DescriptorType`

39   TaskRequirementJustificationItem

Definition
`TaskRequirementJustificationItem` is a <<select>> interface that identifies
items which can be selected as being the source that justifies the `TaskRequirement`.

Reference
- `TaskRequirement`, refer to Para 30

Type
- UML <<select>> stereotype

40   TaskRequirementRevision

Definition
`TaskRequirementRevision` is a <<class>> representing an iteration applied to a
`TaskRequirement`.

Reference
- `TaskRequirement`, refer to Para 30

Type
- UML class

41   taskRequirementRevisionChangeDescription

Definition
`taskRequirementRevisionChangeDescription` is description that gives more
information on content that has been altered between two revisions of a
`TaskRequirement`.

Reference
- `TaskRequirement`, refer to Para 30

Type
- CDM DescriptorType

42 taskRequirementRevisionDate

Definition
taskRequirementRevisionDate is a date that specifies when a
TaskRequirementRevision was defined.

Reference
- TaskRequirementRevision, refer to Para 40

Type
- CDM DateType

43 taskRequirementRevisionIdentifier

Definition
taskRequirementRevisionIdentifier is an identifier that establishes a unique
designator for a TaskRequirementRevision and to differentiate it from other instances
of TaskRequirementRevision.

References
- TaskRequirementRevision, refer to Para 40
- identifier, refer to Chap 2.9

Valid values
- ID (SX001G:taskRequirementRevisionIdentifier)

Type
- CDM IdentifierType

44 taskRequirementRevisionRationale

Definition
taskRequirementRevisionRationale is a description that gives more information
on the justification for revising the TaskRequirement.

Reference
- TaskRequirement, refer to Para 30

Type
- CDM DescriptorType

45 taskRequirementRevisionStatus

Definition
taskRequirementRevisionStatus is a state that identifies the maturity of a
TaskRequirementRevision.

References
- TaskRequirementRevision, refer to Para 40
- state, refer to Chap 2.19

Type
- CDM StateType

46   taskRequirementSpecialResourceRequirement

Definition

`taskRequirementSpecialResourceRequirement` is a description that gives more information on unusual resources which are needed for the performance of the required `Task`.

Reference

- `Task`, refer to Para 5

Type

- CDM `DescriptorType`

47   TaskResource

Definition

`TaskResource` is a <<class>> that identifies means that have to be available to perform a specified amount of work.

Type

- UML class

48   TaskResourceDefinitionItem

Definition

`TaskResourceDefinitionItem` is a <<select>> interface that identifies which items can be used as either infrastructure or material resources.

Type

- UML <<select>> stereotype

49   taskResourceDuration

Definition

`taskResourceDuration` is a property that specifies the average time that a `TaskResource` is needed to perform a specified amount of work.

Reference

- `TaskResource`, refer to Para 47

Type

- CDM `PropertyType`

50   taskResourceIdentifier

Definition

`taskResourceIdentifier` is an identifier that establishes a unique designator for a `TaskResource` and to differentiate it from other instances of `TaskResource`.

References

- `TaskResource`, refer to Para 47
- `identifier`, refer to Chap 2.9

Valid values

- ID (SX001G:taskResourceIdentifier)

Type
- CDM `IdentifierType`

51 TaskResourceItem

Definition
`TaskResourceItem` is an <<extend>> interface that provides its associated data model to those classes that implement it.

Type
- UML <<extend>> stereotype

52 TaskRevision

Definition
`TaskRevision` is a <<class>> representing an iteration applied to a `Task`.

Reference
- `Task`, refer to Para 5

Type
- UML class

53 taskRevisionChangeDescription

Definition
`taskRevisionChangeDescription` is a description that gives more information on content that has been altered between two revisions of a `Task`.

Reference
- `Task`, refer to Para 5

Type
- CDM `DescriptorType`

54 taskRevisionDate

Definition
`taskRevisionDate` is a date that specifies when the `Task` was revised.

Reference
- `Task`, refer to Para 5

Type
- CDM `DateType`

55 taskRevisionIdentifier

Definition
`taskRevisionIdentifier` is an identifier that establishes a unique designator for a `TaskRevision` and to differentiate it from other instances of `TaskRevision`.

References
- `TaskRevision`, refer to Para 52
- `identifier`, refer to Chap 2.9

Valid values
- ID (SX001G:taskRevisionIdentifier)

Type
- CDM `IdentifierType`

56 taskRevisionRationale

Definition
`taskRevisionRationale` is a description that gives more information on the justification for revising the `Task`.

Reference
- `Task`, refer to Para 5

Type
- CDM `DescriptorType`

57 taskRevisionStatus

Definition
`taskRevisionStatus` is a state that identifies the progress on the development of a `TaskRevision`.

References
- `TaskRevision`, refer to Para 52
- `state`, refer to Chap 2.19

Type
- CDM StateType

58 TaskRevisionWarningCautionNote

Definition
`TaskRevisionWarningCautionNote` is a <<relationship>> that identifies a `WarningCautionNote` that is associated with a given `Task`.

References
- `Task`, refer to Para 5
- `WarningCautionNote`, refer to Chap 2.23

Type
- UML class

59 taskTotalLaborTime

Definition
`taskTotalLaborTime` is a property that specifies the total time to be expended during a `Task`.

Note
`taskTotalLaborTime` includes the labor time for all required personnel resources.

Type
- CDM `PropertyType`

60 TaskUsage

Definition

`TaskUsage` is a <<relationship>> that identifies a Task required for the `TaskAnalysisItem`.

References
- `Task`, refer to <u>Para 5</u>
- `TaskAnalysisItem`, refer to <u>Para 8</u>

Type
- UML class

61 TextPropertyType

Definition

`TextPropertyType` is a `PropertyType` that specifies a quantity as a string value.

References
- `PropertyType`, refer to <u>Chap 2.16</u>
- `value`, refer to <u>Chap 2.22</u>

Type
- UML class

62 textValue

Definition

`textValue` is a string of characters that provides the value in text form.

Reference
- `value`, refer to <u>Chap 2.22</u>

Type
- UML string

63 ThreeDimensional

Definition

`ThreeDimensional` is a <<compoundAttribute>> that represents spatial magnitudes.

Type
- UML class

64 ThresholdDefinition

Definition

`ThresholdDefinition` is a <<class>> that represents the circumstance that is used as a trigger or threshold.

Type
- UML class

65 thresholdValue

Definition

`thresholdValue` is a property that represents the value that is measured and evaluated as part of the `ParameterThresholdDefinition`.

References
- ParameterThresholdDefinition, refer to <u>Chap 2.16</u>
- `value`, refer to <u>Chap 2.22</u>

Type
- CDM `PropertyType`

66   thresholdValueQualifier

Definition

`thresholdValueQualifier` is a classification that specifies a constraint to be used when evaluating an actual value against the `thresholdValue`.

References
- `thresholdValue`, refer to <u>Para 65</u>
- `value`, refer to <u>Chap 2.22</u>

Valid values
- B (SX001G:executeBeforeThresholdValueDefinition)
- A (SX001G:executeAfterThresholdValueDefinition)

Type
- CDM `ClassificationType`

67   Time Limit UoF

Definition

The Time Limit UoF provides the capability to define the circumstances under which an action is to be initiated.

68   TimeLimit

Definition

`TimeLimit` is a <<class>> that represents the specification of circumstances under which the associated item is initiated.

Note 1

Time is used in the sense of "time to do something" and must not be seen as only a period of time.

Note 2

`TimeLimit` does not have the concept of an identification, which means that if there is a change to a `TimeLimit` for a `TimeLimitItem`, then all `TimeLimits` must be resent as part of a `Message`.

Type
- UML class

69   timeLimitDescription

Definition

`timeLimitDescription` is a description that provides a human readable expression of the defined time limit expression.

Type
- CDM `DescriptorType`

70   TimeLimitEventItem

Definition

`TimeLimitEventItem` is a <<select>> interface that identifies which items can be used to define an `EventThresholdDefinition`.

Reference

- `EventThresholdDefinition`, refer to Chap 2.5

Type

- UML <<select>> stereotype

71   timeLimitHarmonizationIndicator

Definition

`timeLimitHarmonizationIndicator` is a Boolean that identifies if the `TimeLimit` is the result from a task packaging procedure.

Reference

- `TimeLimit`, refer to Para 68

Type

- UML Boolean

72   TimeLimitItem

Definition

`TimeLimitItem` is an <<extend>> interface that provides its associated data model to those classes that implement it.

Type

- UML <<extend>> stereotype

73   TimeOffset

Definition

`TimeOffset` is an <<attributeGroup>> that specifies an oriented offset from Coordinated Universal Time.

Type

- UML class

74   TimeStampedClassification

Definition

`TimeStampedClassification` is <<compoundAttribute>> that represents a classification in conjunction with its recording time stamp.

Type

- UML class

75   Trade

Definition

Trade is a term that represents a craft or profession which requires specific skills.

References

- Skill, refer to Chap 2.19

Example
- Diesel mechanic is a trade that requires specific mechanical skills

Type
- Business Term

76 Trade

Definition
Trade is a <<class>> that represents a craft or profession which requires specific skills.

Type
- UML class

77 tradeName

Definition
tradeName is a name that uniquely establishes a craft or profession.

Type
- CDM NameType

Chapter 2.21

Glossary - U

Table of contents
Page

List of tables

List of figures

No table of figures entries found.

References

Table 1 References

Chap No./Document No.	Title
Chap 2.2	Glossary - B
Chap 2.9	Glossary - I
Chap 2.16	Glossary - P
Chap 2.22	Glossary - V

1   UML

Definition

Unified Modeling Language.

Type

– Acronym

2 umlBoolean

Definition

`umlBoolean` is a UML-defined primitive that is used for logical expressions, consisting of the predefined values TRUE and FALSE.

Type

– UML class

3 umlInteger

Definition

`umlInteger` is a UML-defined primitive type representing integer values.

Type

– UML class

4 umlReal

Definition

`umlReal` is a UML-defined primitive type representing the mathematical concept of real.

Type

– UML class

5 umlString

Definition

`umlString` is a UML-defined sequence of characters in some suitable character set used to display information about the model. Character sets may include non-Roman alphabets and characters

Note

Character sets may include non-Roman alphabets and characters.

Type

– UML class

6 umlUnlimitedNatural

Definition

`umlUnlimitedNatural` is a UML-defined primitive type representing unlimited natural values.

Type

– UML class

7 unit

Definition

`unit` is a word or a code that identifies the unit of measure in with which the associated quantity values are expressed.

Type

– CDM `validValue`

8 UOF

Definition
Unit of Functionality..

Type
–   Acronym

9 upperBound

Definition
upperBound is a string of characters that represents the upper limit of the range.

Type
–   UML string

10 upperLimitValue

Definition
upperLimitValue is a Real that represents the upper limit of the value range.

Reference
–   value, refer to Chap 2.22

Type
–   UML real

11 upperOffsetValue

Definition
upperOffsetValue is a Real that defines the upper limit variation from the nominal value.

Reference
–   value, refer to Chap 2.22

Type
–   UML real

12 UsableOnItem

Definition
UsableOnItem is an <<extend>> interface that provides its associated data model to those classes that can have a limited effectivity with respect to its usage in one or many instances of ProductVariant.

Reference
–   ProductVariant, refer to Chap 2.16

Type
–   UML <<extend>> stereotype

13 UsableOnProductVariant

Definition
UsableOnProductVariant is a <<relationship>> that defines that a UsableOnItem, included in the Breakdown for the overall Product, is effective in the associated ProductVariant.

Note

UsableOnProductVariant is the equivalent of the Usable On Code in GEIA-0007.

References
- Breakdown, refer to Chap 2.2
- Product, refer to Chap 2.16
- ProductVariant, refer to Chap 2.16
- UsableOnItem, refer to Para 12

Type
- UML class

14   User

Definition

User is a person that has authority to use an item for a specific purpose.

References
- Item, refer to Chap 2.9
- Person, refer to Chap 2.16

Type
- Business Term

Chapter 2.22

Glossary - V

Table of contents
Page

List of tables

References

Table 1 References

Chap No./Document No.	Title
Chap 2.14	Glossary - N
Chap 2.19	Glossary - S

1   value

Definition

`value` is a Real that defines the quantity.

Type

–   UML Real

2   valueDetermination

Definition

`valueDetermination` is a word or a code that qualifies the method by which the value of the property has been determined.

Reference

–   `value`, refer to Para 1

Examples

–   Designed: the value represents a value intended by the design.
–   Set point: the value is used as an initialization value.
–   Measured: the value has been measured.
–   Estimated: the value has been estimated.
–   Calculated: the value has been calculated.

Type
- CDM `validValue`

3 ValueRangePropertyType

Definition

`ValueRangePropertyType` is a `NumericalPropertyType` that specifies a value pair which represents the range limits.

References
- `NumericalPropertyType`, refer to Chap 2.14
- `value`, refer to Para 1

Type
- UML class

4 valueRecordingDateTime

Definition

`valueRecordingDateTime` is a calendar date and time that identifies when the property value was established.

Reference
- `value`, refer to Para 1

Type
- CDM `DateTimeType`

5 ValueWithTolerancesPropertyType

Definition

`ValueWithTolerancesPropertyType` is a `NumericalPropertyType` that specifies a range of values by specifying a single nominal value together with the permitted variations from the nominal value.

References
- `NumericalPropertyType`, refer to Chap 2.14
- `value`, refer to Para 1

Type
- UML class

6 Vendor

Definition
- Refer to supplier, Chap 2.19

Type
- Business Term

Chapter 2.23

Glossary - W

Table of contents
Page

List of tables

References

Table 1 References

Chap No./Document No.	Title
Chap 2.1	Glossary - A
Chap 2.3	Glossary - B
Chap 2.4	Glossary - C
Chap 2.9	Glossary - I

1 Waiver

Definition

Waiver is an authorization granted after execution to depart from a particular performance of the contract, specification or reference document

References

– Authorization, refer to Chap 2.1
– Contract, refer to Chap 2.3
– Document, refer to Chap 2.4

Type

– Business Term

2 WarningCautionNote

Definition

`WarningCautionNote` is a <<class>> that defines advice concerning safety, legal and health aspects.

Type
- UML class

3 warningCautionNoteDescription

Definition
`warningCautionNoteDescription` is a description that gives more information on safety, legal and health considerations.

Type
- CDM `DescriptorType`

4 warningCautionNoteIdentifier

Definition
`warningCautionNoteIdentifier` is an identifier that establishes a unique designator for a warning or caution, and to differentiate it from other instances of warning or caution.

Reference
- `identifier`, refer to Chap 2.9

Valid values
- ID (SX001G:warningCautionNoteIdentifier)

Type
- CDM `IdentifierType`

5 warningCautionNoteType

Definition
`warningCautionNoteType` is a classification that identifies severity and scope for the safety, legal and health considerations.

Valid values
- W (SX001G:warningAdvise)
- C (SX001G:cautionAdvise)
- N (SX001G:noteAdvise)

Type
- CDM `ClassificationType`

6 width

Definition
`width` is a property that specifies the less extended longitudinal dimension of an object.

Type
- CDM `PropertyType`

Chapter 2.24

Glossary - X

Table of contents
Page

List of tables

References

Table 1 References

Chap No./Document No.	Title
None	

1   No glossary entries

No glossary entries begin with the letter X.

Page intentionally blank.

Chapter 2.25

Glossary - Y

Table of contents

Page

List of tables

References

Table 1 References

Chap No./Document No.	Title
Chap 2.22	Glossary - V

1 yearComponent

Definition

`yearComponent` is an Integer that represents the year expressed as a value between '1' and '9999'.

Reference

– `value`, refer to Chap 2.22

Type

– UML integer

Page intentionally blank.

Chapter 2.26

Glossary - Z

Table of contents
Page

List of tables

References

Table 1 References

Chap No./Document No.	Title
Chap 2.2	Glossary - B
Chap 2.16	Glossary - P

1   Zone Element UoF

Definition

The Zone Element UoF defines the characteristics that are unique for a breakdown element that represents a three-dimensional space related to a `Product`.

Reference

- `Product`, refer to Chap 2.16

2   ZoneElement

Definition

`ZoneElement` is a `BreakdownElement` that represents a three-dimensional space related to a `Product`.

Note

A zone can also represent a work area such as a mechanical workshop onboard a ship.

References

- `BreakdownElement`, refer to Chap 2.2
- `Product`, refer to Chap 2.16

Type

- UML class

3 ZoneElementRevision

Definition

`ZoneElementRevision` is a `BreakdownElementRevision` representing an iteration applied to a `ZoneElement`.

References

- `BreakdownElementRevision`, refer to Chap 2.2
- `ZoneElement`, refer to Para 2

Type

- UML class

4 zoneElementType

Definition

`zoneElementType` is a classification that identifies further specialization for a `ZoneElement`.

Reference

- `ZoneElement`, refer to Para 2

Valid values

- W (SX001G:productWorkArea)
- Z (SX001G:productZone)

Type

- CDM ClassificationType

Check out the different specifications in print:

SX000H, *Handbook for the S-Series Integrated Product Support (IPS) Specifications*, Issue 1.0, ISBN 978-84-19125-18-7

SX000i, *International specification for integrated product support (IPS)*, Issue 3.0, ISBN 978-84-19125-19-4

S1000D, *International specification for technical publications using a common source database,* Issue 5.0, (3 volumes), ISBN 978-84-19125-31-6, 978-84-19125-32-3 and 978-84-19125-33-0

S2000M, *International specification for material management - Integrated data processing* Issue 7.0, ISBN 978-84-19125-29-3

S3000L, *International specification for Logistics Support Analysis – LSA*, Issue 2.0, ISBN 978-84-19125-20-0

S4000P, *International specification for developing and continuously improving preventive maintenance*, Issue 2.1, ISBN 978-84-19125-21-7

S5000F, *International specification for in-service data feedback,* Issue 3.0 (2 volumes), ISBNs 978-84-19125-27-9 and 978-84-19125-28-6

S6000T, *International specification for training analysis and design*, Issue 2.0, ISBN 978-84-19125-22-4

SX001G, *Glossary for the S-Series IPS specifications*, Issue 3.0, ISBN 978-84-19125-23-1

SX002D, *Common data model for the S-Series IPS specifications*, Issue 2.1, ISBN 978-84-19125-24-8

SX004G, *UML model reader's guide*, Issue 2.0, ISBN 978-84-19125-25-5

SX005G, *S-Series IPS specifications XML schema implementation guide*, Issue 2.0, ISBN 978-84-19125-26-2

Other books on the S-Series:

Overview of the S-Series IPS specifications, Issue 6.0, by ASD, ISBN 978-84-19125-02-6

Further books on the S-Series to be published by Editorial Dragon:

An introduction to the S-Series IPS specifications by Ramón Somoza, ISBN 978-84-19125-16-3

S-Series data models and XML schemas by Ramón Somoza, ISBN 978-84-19125-17-0